Belief and Unbelief

Books by the Same Author:

THE EXPERIENCE OF MARRIAGE: (Editor)
THE OPEN CHURCH
A NEW GENERATION
THE TIBER WAS SILVER

Belief
and Unbelief

A Philosophy of Self-Knowledge

MICHAEL NOVAK

The Macmillan Company, New York

WITHDRAWN

THEODORE LOWNIK LIBRARY
BENEDICTINE UNIVERSITY
5700 COLLEGE ROAD
LISLE, IL 60532-0900

121.6
N85b

Copyright © Michael Novak 1965
All rights reserved. No part of this book
may be reproduced or utilized in any form
or by any means, electronic or mechanical,
including photocopying, recording or by
any information storage and retrieval
system, without permission in writing from
the Publisher.
Fourth Printing 1966
The Macmillan Company, New York
Collier-Macmillan Canada Ltd., Toronto, Ontario
Library of Congress catalog card number: 65-22611
PRINTED IN THE UNITED STATES OF AMERICA

For Karen's parents and for mine
GEORGE AND MARY LAUB
MICHAEL AND IRENE NOVAK
with affection and gratitude

ACKNOWLEDGMENTS

The author wishes to thank the following for permission to reproduce copyrighted material: New Directions for the line "Do not go gentle into that good night" from *The Collected Poems of Dylan Thomas*, copyright © 1953 by Dylan Thomas, copyright © 1957 by New Directions, reprinted by permission of the publishers, New Directions, New York, J. M. Dent & Sons, Ltd., London; George Braziller, Inc. for *The Words* by Jean-Paul Sartre, published in England by Longman & Todd; *Commonweal* for a review by Thomas Merton of *Honest to God* by J. A. T. Robinson, in the August 1964 issue; Basil Blackwell and Mott, Ltd. for "Systematically Misleading Expressions" by Gilbert Ryle from *Essays in Logic and Language*; and for *Three Philosophers* by G. E. M. Anscombe and P. T. Geach; New York University Press for *Religious Experience and Truth* by Sidney Hook; Alfred A. Knopf, Inc. for Albert Camus, *The Fall*, and Henry David Aiken, "God and Evil," in *Reason and Conduct*; Simon and Schuster, Inc. for Paul Edwards' introduction to *Why I Am Not a Christian* by Bertrand Russell; Charles Scribner's Sons for *The Nature and Destiny of Man* by Reinhold Niebuhr; Viking Press for Ben Ray Redman's introduction to *The Portable Voltaire*; Student Christian Movement Press, Ltd. and The Macmillan Co. for "Can God's Existence be Disproved?" in *New Essays in Philosophical Theology* by Antony Flew and Alasdair MacIntyre; The Macmillan Co. for *Science and Human Behavior* by B. F. Skinner, *Intellectual Autobiography* by Reinhold Niebuhr, and for *Reinhold Niebuhr: His Religious, Social and Political Thought* edited by Charles W. Kegley and Robert W. Bretall; St Martin's Press, Inc. for *The Quest for Being* by Sidney Hook.

CONTENTS

Contents

FOREWORD

"Atheism is a cruel and long-range affair," Jean-Paul Sartre writes in *The Words*. "I think I've carried it through."[1] But now that he has carried his project through, how does his state of mind differ from a believer's? Is atheism a more truthful, more human project?

How does one answer such questions, faced with the prospect of a single, short life which it is necessary to live well? One does not want to misconceive the nature of life; one does not want to choose badly. What direction shall one take? In the end one's decision springs from, and determines, who one is. An inquiry preceding such a decision requires clarity about one's starting place.

I was born a Catholic, and many times that fact has prompted me to alternate between gratitude and despair: gratitude because I am quite sure that if I had not been born a Catholic I would scarcely have found my way into the Church. Like a certain French philosopher, I would have thought of it as "that dunghill." I have often felt despair because God came to me too easily, before I had a chance, entering my blood and bones through my mother's milk. It might have been easier to decide freely whether to believe or to disbelieve if I had been born an atheist.

There are many things in the atheistic position that I envy, and struggle to make my own. But always there have been contrary experiences and reflections that made it impossible for me to become an atheist conscientiously.

The reflections which preoccupied my mind as I labored to complete this inquiry in the summer of 1964 concerned the Negro revolution in America, the workings of the Second Vatican Council in Rome the preceding autumn, and the assassination of President Kennedy. The first of these impressed upon me with great clarity how irrelevant religion can be in the daily struggles of men for compassion and justice. Many who bore the brunt of the racial struggle, giving of their blood and their integrity of life and limb, had no need of religious inspiration. What did they lack, these moralists and doers, that religious men might boast?

The preceding autumn had brought me a profound sense of the human weakness of the Catholic Church, assembled in Council. Such reflections were not new to me, but they struck me with great, deep, steady force. Some few men who still wield great intellectual and spiritual leadership in the Church appeared to be puny, often benighted, and certainly limited human beings. The degree to which they are prisoners of certain historic forms, ceremonials, patterns of judgment, and aspirations could not escape an honest eye. Why should one's salvation be bound up with men of such inconsiderable stature, with minds and spirits that offer so little to admire? There were many outstanding and attractive men in Rome, to be sure. But the quality of those few who had for so long held so much power in the Church depressed me more than the promise held out by the many. If the leadership of the Church had been involved in such mediocrity for several generations, why should one take it seriously, or commit one's life to it?

I returned from Rome to the United States in January, 1964, weary and exhausted by the strain of meeting a close deadline on my report upon the Council. The news that met me immediately upon arrival was that my younger brother, a priest in Pakistan, was missing in the violent riots near Dacca, and was presumed dead. I knew he was dead. As the reports became more definite, the details were only crueler than I had expected. He had been challenged by several thugs, for no apparent reason, was stabbed several times, and his body either left to pariah dogs or buried secretly and irretrievably. His clothing, glasses, and bicycle were later found; there was reason to believe that officials knew the fate of the corpse but refused to reveal it.

The murder was senseless. It seemed as useless as that of President Kennedy, which had preceded it by exactly eight weeks. It was not, however, the emotional shock but a cumulative weariness that oppressed me. I became aware of human fragility, the need for absolute reliance upon conscience and determination, the uselessness of illusions, props, or "extra" or "super" faiths. We are what we are, we do what we do. It is not at all certain that it makes any difference to our identity whether there is a God, a heaven, and all the so-useless paraphernalia of a church. Without these things, some men do as well as others do who have them. And even if one has them, they are of no comfort when pure and naked faith before an inscrutable God is called for. Masses for the dead are small consolation when one is numb and all the patterns of security have been fractured. They mean something only if there is a God. But if there is, his ways are so foreign to men's that the visible liturgy of men is next to meaningless unless one already believes. And that is the very point in question.

In any case, when one's faith has been beaten and winnowed, and when one finds oneself saying, not knowing how, "Though he will slay me, yet will I love him," then the project of belief seems to be as cruel and long-range as Sartre has found unbelief to be. And one is left with the same practical, daily necessities as Sartre. There is no comfort in the heart, no oil upon the forehead, or ointment on one's wounds. There is no vision of a heaven nor any haven of hope. One lowers one's head, unfeeling, and does what one has to do. What is there to do but go on, seeing a little more clearly, having fewer illusions, knowing better the limited jobs one has to do? Sartre describes the task of writing in terms one can only accept: "It's a habit, and besides,

it's my profession. For a long time, I took my pen for a sword;
I now know we're powerless. No matter. I write and will keep
writing books . . . my sole concern has been to save myself . . .
nothing in my hands, nothing up my sleeves—by work and
faith."[2]

My brother, at twenty-eight, was the first priest to study
Arabian philosophy at Dacca University, after generations of
Christian and Moslem isolation. Many Moslems were delighted
by his interest, and he himself was beginning to look at Christianity with Eastern eyes. For a moment the future seemed to be
opening. Yet it is futile to count on success in history.

I now see that there is nothing to do but work. One must do
one's best, unable to control the consequences or set the limits
of one's fate. Like Sartre, I "relegate salvation to the proproom,"
not understanding in the least what is meant by the word. Yet,
unlike him, I do not call salvation "impossible." It is simply that
I do not understand God, nor the way in which he works. Perhaps there is a heaven, and I will see my brother, together with
his murderers. That is beyond my ken. I only know that my
salvation lies in fidelity to conscience, in fidelity to my work,
in fidelity to those I love, in whatever contribution I can make
toward diminishing the amount of suffering in this world. I do
not think about the end; I attend to each task at its appointed
time. If, occasionally, I raise my heart in prayer, it is to no God
I can see, or hear, or feel. It is to a God in as cold and obscure
a polar night as any nonbeliever has known. God is no "extra"
in my life. My nose is at my tasks. With a naked belief I believe
that such fidelity is not in vain, not a mere spark of sense in a
suffocating universe, but the key and important fact within man's
range of knowledge. I am prepared to admit that my belief may
be wrong; I set no special store by it. My obligation is to be
faithful to my conscience, and I do not expect that I would
hesitate an instant once it was clear to me that atheism is a more
consistent human policy. A conscience faithful till death is of

more importance than being on a certain side, whether of belief or unbelief.

A word about this inquiry: the attempt to complete it has met countless interruptions. At least ten times more pages than here appear have been written and discarded, since the first draft made in 1960. I wish the final product showed a precision and a polish justifying the several rewritings. But I am afraid the final draft is even more different from the one preceding it than the latter was from its predecessor. The manner of proceeding, perhaps, has improved if the finish of the prose has not.

Finally, I could not have completed this book without the severe, bracing, and helpful criticisms of Richard Roelofs of the Department of Philosophy at the University of Rochester. Over the years many other friends have helped me correct mistakes or forced me to raise further questions—Daniel Callahan and David Burrell especially.

My wife Karen suffered with me through long summers spent mainly indoors at work on this book. Valentine Rice, the Reverend Frederick Crowe, S.J., Robert Schrader, Thomas Tymoczko, and several others read the manuscript and made useful suggestions. Mrs. Muriel Goodridge, Mrs. Patricia Thompson, and Miss Ann Murphy helped with typing, bibliography, and related tasks.

MICHAEL NOVAK

Cambridge, Massachusetts
December, 1964

INTRODUCTION:
A DIALECTICAL INQUIRY

1. Toward Civil Conversation

This book is an attempt to work out some of the problems of
self-identity, and some of the problems of belief and unbelief.
The roots of the two sets of problems are entangled. For in
deciding who one is, one relates oneself to others, to the world,
and to God. If there is a God, one approach to human life is
fitting. If there is not a God, another approach makes its demands.
But there seem to be many men today—and their numbers constantly increase—who both believe and disbelieve, who are not
agnostics but who recognize in their hearts a divided allegiance.
Through all their busy activities for the betterment of men, they
keep "an open mind" regarding a power or an intelligence they
do not dare to call "God." "Ah, *mon cher*," Albert Camus has
written, "for anyone who is alone, without God and without a
master, the weight of days is dreadful. Hence one must choose
a master, God being out of style. Besides, that word has lost its
meaning. . . . Take our moral philosophers, for instance, so
serious, loving their neighbor and all the rest—nothing distinguishes them from Christians, except that they don't preach in
churches."[1]

Among such nonbelievers, the question of God has not been
dismissed. Among such believers, doubts are persistent. Many
men today are divided men, if not in their commitments yet
nevertheless in their intellectual theories. Who can say, to his

own or anyone's satisfaction, what it is thoroughly to believe? or thoroughly to disbelieve? Most of us borrow our values where we find them, since a thorough atheistic humanism has not yet been worked out.

Yet it is impossible for one who believes in God to work in the intellectual world of the United States without becoming aware that among intellectuals the bias of the age leans in quite the opposite direction. A great many of one's philosophical associates, and certainly the most articulate, are agnostics or atheists.[2] One need not drift with the stream, of course. Those who believe in God are now, by a new turn of the conventional wisdom, the chief bearers of the tradition of dissent.

But why does one believe? What is the basis of one's belief, its root and its dynamic? And what prevents one from joining the numbers of those who have ceased to believe?

These questions are not easy to answer, not only because they deal with matters difficult in themselves, but because the language of science and common sense systematically excludes reference to experiences fundamental to belief, and because the traditional language of our religious culture is now bankrupt. The aim of the present inquiry, however, is not so much to propose a new vocabulary for belief, however seriously that task requires to be done, as to focus attention upon the direction from which that vocabulary must spring. The contribution this study hopes to make, then, is: (1) to have staked out for further inquiries a fruitful vein of human experience; and, more specifically, (2) to have begun the hard work of elucidating those experiences of human intellectual life in which belief in God is rooted; that is, the experiences of "intelligent subjectivity."

The phrase "intelligent subjectivity" represents the central point of this book. Nevertheless, to offer a definition of it here would almost surely prompt the reader to misunderstand it. For to call attention to intelligent subjectivity is not to call attention to a new concept, a new formula, a new use of words, which once memorized has been mastered. It is to ask the reader to discover certain facets of his inquiring, thinking, and knowing that he has perhaps seldom reflected upon. It is to ask the reader to attend to his own intellectual activities—for example, as he reads the pages of this inquiry. Our study, then, is not an inquiry into the use of the words "intelligent subjectivity," nor into the meaning of the concept "intelligent subjectivity." It is an exercise in *using* intelligent subjectivity. It is an inquiry into how the reader, and the writer, inquire. It is an inquiry into the real cognitional life of the reader, and of the writer. At the end of the inquiry, each should know more about *himself*, and not merely have added a new phrase to his vocabulary.

By "subjectivity," then, I mean to call attention to what the reader—and the writer—does, as a conscious subject rather than as an object. I mean to call attention to those experiences of personal life which cannot, technically, be observed, either by others or by oneself. For to observe is to regard an object, and the self as subject is not to be discovered as an object is discovered. The experiences which we have of ourselves as subjects emerge in our awareness without our looking for them or at them. They are not observed, although they may upon demand be adverted to and analyzed.

By "intelligent" I wish to emphasize that these experiences of the subject are not emotional, nor "of the heart"; rather, they are proper to our intellectual life. I have been anxious to avoid as much as possible the fashionable new language of "encounter" or of "I-thou," wishing instead to work out a more empirical and intellectualist approach to belief. By focusing attention on intelligent subjectivity, then, I hope to have succeeded in calling attention to an obvious part of our experience which is properly described neither as emotive nor as cognitive, in the sense that present usage generally ascribes to these words.

Nevertheless, this inquiry is addressed to the general reader rather than to the professional philosopher—to that general reader who has ever been the lifeblood of Anglo-American philosophy. The professionals, I hope, will look kindly on my efforts to attain clarity in a neglected and difficult area of discussion, and find some of my emphases or distinctions of interest. But it was ever the lay reader whom I tried to keep in mind as I prepared the final draft, whose interest in the decision between belief and unbelief may be presumed to be as keen as my own. I have not the faintest hope of convincing anybody, one way or the other, and even less of solving all the technical problems of both belief and unbelief from a philosophical and ethical point of view. But if this inquiry has singled out, in intelligent subjectivity, a fruitful and perhaps the basic area of disagreement, then it may perhaps have opened a way for believers and nonbelievers to speak seriously and civilly with one another. For as matters now stand, the one word one does not use in serious conversation without upsetting someone is "God"—unless in the context the word has been domesticated and rendered by mutual agreement rather meaningless.

2. The Attraction of Atheism

Atheism is an attractive policy of life; but is it consistent with intelligence and love?[3] There is something compelling in the vision of Prometheus, chained to rocks, defying the gods. It is satisfying sometimes to rage openly—"Do not go gentle into that good night." The indifference of the Anglo-American pragmatist is also attractive; although his indifference to religion is a marvel a believer can but envy from afar and practice only upon occasion. A believer might sometime enjoy the inner conviction, presently appropriated by the nonbeliever, that he is deciding bravely who he is and what he shall be for the sixty years or so of consciousness allotted him on earth. He might like to share in the honesty, courage, and integrity which in our time the nonbeliever attributes only to himself. He is sometimes attracted by the myth that spiritually men are isolated individuals. For then he would have no Church to carry on his back, and would not feel each of the historical sins of the Church as a needle driven into his flesh.

Perhaps there is no God at all in the deep point of his consciousness. Perhaps a habit of mind not yet uprooted deceives him. Going to Church or saying "Lord!" is no guarantee that belief resides at the core of one's spirit. What is the guarantee?

A believer tries to imagine himself an atheist. But always, when he has as a model an atheist whom he admires—M. Sartre, or even more, M. Camus—for a few days he has their emptiness, their polar night. And then it occurs to him, that that same night is the God he had fled. In M. Sartre and in M. Camus, he finds the image of what he wants to be. He does as they do—except that he does not find it effective, so far as God is concerned.

Thus, he keeps finding that after all he does believe in God. Sometimes he is even certain that he knows him, that he loves him. Do not ask him how; there is no proof. He sits here under a lamp, in August, 1964, pen in hand. He is sure: there it is. And yet it is only partly his serenity that tells him he believes; it is even more his inability to believe any countervailing arguments in the face of that serenity. No atheist he has ever read has helped him cut the roots of his belief in God. The gods they have destroyed have sometimes startled him by the noise of their crumbling. But he was ever sure these were not God. "Nietzsche is dead" he has seen scrawled in crayon upon a billboard; "(signed) God."

Many a believer feels out of step with others in his generation. He neither believes with the believers, nor disbelieves with the atheists. He is not an agnostic; it is not fear nor hesitation that inhibits him. He goes on writing, and reflecting. His happiness, and his salvation, lie in his work. If he is true to his conscience, he will be "saved," one way or the other.

But whether that "salvation" will usher him into the Face of

God he does not know. Will there be silence? Nothing at all? What could a God possibly be like? Had he not been born a believer perhaps such questions would not bother him. The "linguistic therapy" offered by some philosophers, in any case, has failed to cure him. Their scalpels and their tiny lights do not touch the area of intelligence in which his questions breed. They seem to speak a simpler, more puritan language than he has ever heard. They have too long spoken of God as someone else's problem, a distant memory, a disease.

The origin of his difficulties lies doubtless in a decision made long ago to live between two worlds, not as one in doubt, but as one to whom the usual resources of comfort on both sides have been closed. The securities of believers are easily unmasked by nonbelievers; and those of nonbelief, by believers. The believer remains in the part of his conscience where belief and unbelief war. Fidelity to conscience is his comfort, full of illusions and infidelities, yet self-corrective. Such fidelity does not lead decisively to "truth" or "error." He is a practicing believer, in many ways an enthusiastic believer, in all ways his own kind of believer. Yet he feels spiritually far closer to men like Albert Camus than to many a bishop and theologian. And that closeness establishes the problem to be examined in this book.

How does unbelief differ from belief? In each man, elements of both remain. It is a legitimate prayer for a believer to say, "Lord, help my unbelief." And it is becoming common to hear an unbeliever cautiously admit: "Some things are *as if* there were a God." In our generation there appears to be a crisis of unbelief, as years ago there was a crisis of belief. The unbeliever speaks of his temptation to succumb to "a failure of nerve." Young people, brought up by nonbelieving parents, are raising again the question of God, just as their parents, brought up by believing parents, cleansed their minds of it. On the other hand, many young believers, the first in their families to receive a college education, or at least to take education seriously, are tempted by nonbelief. Scandalized and repelled by the institutional church and by a world view fashioned in a bygone age, they encounter too few authentic believers who, furthermore, can understand their restlessness. They admire and emulate the life of the good nonbeliever, the secular saint. Belief and unbelief —the double attraction of our age.

The more one has lost one's illusions—the more, St. John of the Cross would say, one's faith advances from the human tokens of faith to the Uncreated, whose mode of presence is emptiness and nothingness—the less impressive is the rhetoric of the churches, the causes and the comforts of institutional belief. Inevitably, one stands before God, and God is silent. He does not show himself to any man in his lifetime, at least not in a way that can influence the decision of one who does not believe. Unless one already believes, there is no "revelation." This is not a question of temporal priorities; it is a question of the structure of communion with God. The instant a believer "sees," he at once "believes." Revelation and belief are mutually constitutive. In this sense belief and unbelief have nothing to say to one another. One sees, or one does not see. Being irreligious is like being tone-deaf or color-blind. But the question remains whether it is the religious or the irreligious who see correctly; perhaps the religious perceive what is not there.

On the other hand, a man's own experience of belief cannot be taken from him merely because others disbelieve. His obscure, inarticulable experience of God (if such he interprets it to be) may have meaning only for him. But it may have a great deal of meaning for him—so much so that it outweighs all challenges brought against it. In another area of discourse, the same situation arises. A group of philosophers with a certain limited theory about what it is to know may hold that a man cannot be certain that he perceives his own hand in front of his face. For anyone who accepts their idea of what knowing is, what certainty is, and what perception is, their position, however discommodious, is unassailable. And yet it will always be open to a Mr. Green to say, as a harbinger of philosophical renewal: "But I *do* know that my hand is in front of my face and, confound it, I have no more certain knowledge than that." He may even say this before he is able to work out a new theory of knowing, of certainty, and of perception that will justify his saying it.

A belief that one has experienced God counts only for the person who holds that belief; and there are many reasons why a man who cherishes such a belief should be on guard against illusions. The believer often fails to recognize that he needs a criterion for distinguishing in himself true belief as opposed to false; he needs a way of guarding against illusions; he needs a method of "testing the spirit." We can go even further: a man who believes he believes in God may require another belief to assure himself that he *truly* believes in God. For perhaps he has only inherited certain reflexes, certain emotional responses, certain conceptual frameworks, just as he once inherited a belief in Santa Claus that explained the mysteries of Christmas. How does one know that one's belief is truly in *God*, not merely in some habitual emotion or pattern of response? How does one convince oneself that one in fact believes in God—merely by repeating the words and feeling a certain emotion? It is difficult for some persons to ascertain whether they have ever actually believed in God, though they have often performed religious acts and thought religious thoughts.

It would be possible to object to M. Sartre, moreover, that he sells belief far too short. As his authentic atheism is a long-range project, so is authentic belief. No one who has come to authentic belief, beyond earlier illusions, thinks of God as a railway conductor who examines one's ticket, inquires about one's destination, and determines one's right to be met safely at the end of the line.[4] The true God is no all-seeing eye scrutinizing one's secret conduct, like the projection of an overactive superego.[5] If one believes in God—the true God and no created counterfeit—there is no consolation and no terror to be derived from dreams about a watching, inquiring, waiting authority in a functionary's uniform. No such image manifests the content of authentic belief in God; no image whatsoever represents the object of such belief.

It is for this reason that the believer can never be certain that his belief is accurate and true; he must go out into a great night of his senses, imagination, and intelligence, and cling with naked adherence to a God he cannot clearly apprehend. The believer who thinks carefully about his belief has placed himself in a darkness as intense as that of the nonbeliever. His world view and his actions may be very different (or they may not be). But he is no more comforted or consoled than the nonbeliever by the course of the world or of his life. He does not hold within his fist the mystery of human life. He is held in darkness by a hidden God.

Stripped of all consolation—as he sometimes, even often, is—the believer can only continue to do what he knows he must do. He tries to do it well. He can count on no assurance but that of his own conscience that he is on the right path in his work. He places one foot in front of the other as best he can. He eats but the crumbs of peace. If his peace sometimes surpasses understanding, so at other times does his emptiness.

Yet it would be less than honest to say that the believer does not know a precious serenity, often hardly detectable beneath the stress of his poverty of spirit and his uncertainty. It is a serenity that comes from fidelity to the deepest instincts of his conscience, a fidelity in the acceptance of darkness and distress. It is a Yes to the universe and the unseen God, the Yes Ivan Karamazov could not say to both at once, a Yes even to the cruel and irrational suffering of human life. It is a reconciliation such as M. Sartre manifests, knowing that the world is not glibly changed: "I now know we're powerless. . . . Culture doesn't save anything or anyone, it doesn't justify."[6] It is the reconciliation of Matthew Arnold choosing Dante's "In His will, our peace," as the most noble line in human poetry. For the nonbeliever, the reconciliation may be sad or fatalistic. It may be merely an aged, wise refusal to rage like an adolescent against nonexistent gods. For the believer, the reconciliation is more than that. It brings a secret, light, restful joy. It brings a serenity that measures blind power, cruelty, and indiscriminate suffering for what they are, often enough drains them to the bitter dregs, does not fathom why they are, yet continues to trust that they are the disguises of love.

The believer need not forgive God for the suffering of this world; like Job, he may accuse God to his face. But he does not cease to remain faithful to the conscience which cautions him not, finally, to be dismayed. Belief in God, he knows, could be an empty illusion, even a crime against his own humanity. He knows the stakes. If he is faithful to his conscience and thinks clearly concerning what he is about, he has no place in his heart for complacency or that sweet pseudoreligious "peace" that sickens honest men. His belief is not unsteady—quite the contrary—though he knows that the thread supporting it, however firmly, is so slender that in the night it cannot by any means be seen. This commitment to conscience keeps him faithful, and his daily experience may make his commitment as plausible as Sartre's experience made his, but there is no final way short of death of proving who is right. Each man has but a single life, during which his choice may go either way. That choice affects many things in his life, but one thing it does not affect: his reliance on his own conscience (formed, no doubt, in friendship with other men) as his sole concern and comfort.

No one has seen God.

3. *The Task of Our Inquiry*

This book, we have said, is an attempt to work out some problems of self-identity. Its aim is to provide empirical tools for sorting out the elements of belief and unbelief in one's own mind. (For how shall we begin to answer: Who am I? Is there a God? What shall I hope for? How shall I live?) It hopes to provide tools for coming to grips with oneself. To this end, it must first try to create a more adequate language than we yet have at hand.

Most of the pages in this book must thus be given to an inquiry into the recurrent experiences of intelligent subjectivity. Such an inquiry is basic to a discussion of belief and unbelief, all the more so because it has long been neglected by philosophers. Serious belief in God, or serious unbelief, arise from decisions made consciously, intelligently, and for oneself. Such decisions are subjective in the sense that they alter the inner life of their subject. They alter his view of himself, his relations to others and to the world, and even his use of the common word "God." But such decisions are intelligent or rational in proportion as the subject can give reasons for the decision that he makes.

Intelligent subjectivity, however, is operative in a very large range of human actions. There are many ways in which intelligence influences our theoretical and our practical decisions, in the sciences, in politics, in friendship, in concrete pragmatic action. Our present philosophical skills do not allow us to articulate these influences clearly. Michael Polanyi, in *Personal Knowledge*,[7] has spelled out some of them. Bernard Lonergan, in *Insight: A Study of Human Understanding*,[8] has spelled out others. But even those who have not wrestled with these large and difficult volumes are often aware, as they listen to the lectures or read the books of many scientists and philosophers, that more things are wrought by human intelligence than men can yet speak well about. Concerning intelligent consciousness, in short, we are still at a rudimentary stage of human speech. We make facile and unsatisfactory distinctions between "emotive" and "cognitive," "rational" and "irrational," "reasons of the reason" and "reasons of the heart," "objective" and "subjective"; whereas, in fact, most of our important decisions in life—whether concerning the canons and criteria of rationality in our sciences, or concerning the general criteria and concrete decisions of our practical actions—depend on the exercise of intelligent subjectivity. At the root of the fundamental acts of human life lies the making of intelligent decisions. The ancient name for making such decisions well is wisdom.

Philosophy is love of wisdom. It is also the study of intelligent subjectivity—not in the abstract, but in the actuality of one's own life. What good would it do one's self to be able to recite distinctions important to intelligent subjectivity, if one could not exercise its realities in one's own life? Philosophy is primarily self-knowledge. Perhaps that is why philosophers who imitate mathematicians, or physicists, or linguists, are tempted to think that philosophy no longer has a function, and why certain ways of "doing" philosophy seem to be like playing games with words.

At the root of one's inquiries into one's own identity, however, the question of God inevitably arises. The fact of human consciousness is a surprising fact in the universe as we now know it. A man is not like a tree, a planet, or a cat[9]—a fact that once reflected upon brings the inquirer up short. There are ways, of course, to dissipate this surprise. One can study human consciousness "objectively," "from the outside," to observe its effects in other men, to generalize about it in the abstract. Human consciousness seems then like any other phenomenon. But as soon as one becomes oneself again, aware of oneself, and content to reflect upon this awareness and its implications, the surprise— and a new set of questions—emerges once again. Philosophy begins with such surprises.

It is difficult to regiment oneself as one would plant a tree or train a cat. It is difficult to condition oneself as thoroughly as one can condition mice in a cage. For there seems always to remain the option between this way of conditioning and that other way, between making a new effort and simply drifting with the present current. As soon as one gains insight into a pattern of conditioning already operative in one's life, one seems to have the primary option of inventing another pattern, and then the further options (*i*) of deciding whether to favor the old pattern or the new, and (*ii*) of making an effort to continue the old or to initiate the new.

One contemporary way of getting at this sense of personal consciousness is through an analysis of the use of the first-person (and/or second-person) pronouns in our language. To speak of a person present in one's group as "him," "her," "someone," or "it" is—in certain contexts of friendly discourse—an insult, if, for example, the implication is that the person referred to is an unwanted eavesdropper. Martin Buber[10] and Gabriel Marcel[11] have independently explored such human facts. William Poteat,[12] Ian T. Ramsey,[13] and Stuart Hampshire[14] have variously explored first-person language and other basic considerations in religious and ethical contexts.

But a more direct way of coming to an understanding of one's own personal consciousness is by learning certain techniques of self-understanding which are subject to empirical controls and intersubjective testing. If a man says, for example, that he gets the point of a joke—he laughed when everyone else did—we may ask him what he thought was funny. We come to know ourselves, and to test our self-knowledge, as members of an articulate community, not as isolated consciousness. Thus introspection and public discourse fecundate one another. The original creative man is nourished by, goes beyond, and then, in turn, nourishes the ongoing life of his community.[15]

A philosophy of the human subject, then, relies upon that self-understanding by which each person consciously appropriates his own intelligent subjectivity; and yet it is subject to public and empirical controls. The situation of such a philosophy exactly matches the situation of men: one can lead a man to freedom, but no one can make him free; one can talk about intelligent subjectivity, but only the subject can exercise it. There are public and empirical signposts, distinctions, and controls that enable individual men to come to understand their own intelligent subjectivity, but only the individual can come to exercise that understanding himself. It is possible, under satisfactory conditions, for others to judge by a man's behavior whether he has made such a self-appropriation.[16] But there is no possible way for one man to make it for another.

There are four activities experienced by the human subject which it seems crucial to be able to recognize in oneself, in their exercise and in their implications: awareness, insight, reflective consciousness, and the drive to understand. There are, of course, countless other experiences it would be well to recognize in oneself, but these four will prove especially important. Moreover, it does not matter what names one gives these experiences; what matters is that they be recognized for what they are, by whatever names one calls them. I have chosen names as best I can, in the hope of accurate communication; but each reader must show generosity in looking for the experiences intended, and in not being blocked by objections he might have to my choice of names.

Nowhere is communication more difficult than in the search— with another—for one's own identity. We are each victims of certain sets of words, certain points of view. It is very difficult for us to follow an argument in which another person uses our favorite words in a pejorative way, and our damning words with favor. "Reason" or "science," for example, invite suspicion from some persons, loyalty from others; "pragmatism" is noble to some and ignoble to others; "intuition" is the secret of life, or the chief source of illusion, to different persons. Yet it often turns out that the experiences to which persons refer by their different use of words are strikingly similar; men are sometimes kept apart more by words, than by realities. In coming to understand ourselves, we should attend primarily to our own experiences, to words only secondarily, lest screens of words separate us even from ourselves.

The main contribution such a book as this can hope to make, then, is to turn attention to an overlooked area of human experience. Such an attempt, initially at least, recommends itself, since a philosophy which springs from new self-knowledge renews itself at almost every point. For when a man knows that he knows, and knows better what his knowing is, then there is every likelihood that he will avoid many mistakes in what he claims to know; his epistemology, his metaphysics, his philosophy of science, art, and politics, and his ethics flow from a clearer stream.

In the second place, when a man seeks to know who he is, he enters into the universe of religious discourse. His inquiry may not be explicitly religious, but he is at least engaged upon the soil in which religious inquiry takes root.

4. A Dialectical, Not Formal, Mode

There is a special temptation for Christians living after the Enlightenment to try to spell out their experience in the language of the Enlightenment. To succumb to that temptation is to invite failure.[17] From the time of Descartes onward (Pascal[18] said he would never forgive Descartes for speaking of God in this language) a special class of interpretations has surrounded the word "reason," such that anyone who begins to use the language of intelligence according to that class of interpretations must end by placing "reason" and "faith" on opposite sides of a divide. There are many things about belief in God that cannot be said in words dear to the Enlightenment. There are many experiences of human life which are spoken of only with great difficulty, if at all, in the systems clustering around the various canons of "reason" employed by post-Cartesian philosophers. To every age of philosophers some debt is owed; but each age also has its deficiencies. One deficiency not yet met by philosophers is the lack of a suitable language for talking about intelligent subjectivity.

Such a language would make it much easier to speak about

belief in God. For, formally, deciding to believe in God is in many respects like deciding to accept certain canons of rationality. There is no way of demonstrating that such canons are necessary, though one may offer reasons for choosing one set rather than another. One cannot compel their acceptance, though one can show their acceptance to result in certain fruits. A man does not commit himself to fidelity to scientific method by a priori necessity; for not all men do so commit themselves. Yet such commitment of one's entire intellectual energy is not merely arbitrary. Like belief in God in another age, however, it may be made without much critical reflection, merely as a matter of course.

No doubt, even if a language for speaking about intelligent subjectivity comes into common use, it will still be impossible to speak adequately about God. Yet one must do what one can. It is as natural to try to express one's beliefs as it is for a child to make sounds before he has learned to talk. We must speak of him; yet when we do, we babble: *"Balbutiendo ut possumus excelsa Dei resonamus."*[19] No one who believes in the true God (and in no counterfeit) thinks that he can talk well about him. On the other hand, if any language is even remotely useful for talking about God, the likelihood is that it will be the language by which we speak of intelligent subjectivity. For God is believed to be at least more like men than like any other thing in the universe about which men can speak.

Finally, many of the themes in this book will be reminiscent of points made by Reinhold Niebuhr and Paul Tillich, though my own intellectual orientation is not as marked as theirs by studies in German idealism and classical rationalism. My main intellectual debt, instead, is probably to Bernard Lonergan. His influence will be felt in nearly every chapter, though he himself may well be a severe critic of my inquiry.

For ultimately this book is personal. The question of belief and unbelief cannot, in the end, be discussed in a formal way.

Through many failures in what may be called (though not in Carnap's sense) the formal mode, I came to see that the philosophical form required is what Kierkegaard called "an edifying discourse," a form which engages each reader in an inquiry into his own identity. For God, as we shall come to see, is the objective not of our concepts and our syllogisms but of our intentionality, and thus is not enclosed in our formal systems. Undoubtedly, some professional philosophers will look askance at a form so little used in the schools. Yet one can ask their forbearance, and hope that a better formalist will succeed on that level which the formal mode can reach, as Lonergan has succeeded for certain of his readers.

Nevertheless, the structure of the problem under inquiry works against the formal mode. Even if a man should come to get all his definitions straight and to use the proper technical words correctly and in their proper relationships, still he will not yet have succeeded in coming to grips with *his own* intelligent subjectivity, nor gained insight into the way God is come upon and spoken of by men, nor yet made a free act of belief or disbelief in God. Unless that insight has been gained and that choice made, words in the formal mode are like words in a foreign language. Neither belief nor unbelief is the conclusion to a syllogism.

The problem on which this inquiry is attempting to throw light is that of the radical similarities and dissimilarities between atheism and belief, in order that intelligent decisions can be made, and in order that believers and nonbelievers can begin to speak intelligently to one another. This inquiry forecloses no questions, but tries to locate them in their proper area. It tries to enter that part of human experience where belief and unbelief thrive together, and contend for possession.

Belief and Unbelief

I ❖

THE CULTURAL CONTEXT

1. The "Post-Religious" Age

No man believes, or disbelieves, in isolation; he believes in the context of a certain historical community. Moreover, belief and unbelief draw their concrete meaning from the life of a particular community. There are no abstract essences "belief" and "unbelief." There are only changing historical realities of different types.[1] One cannot understand the belief of John Locke, the unbelief of David Hume, the belief of Bishop Butler, the unbelief of John Stuart Mill, the belief of Madame Sartre or the unbelief of her son, the belief of American Protestants and the unbelief of American intellectuals, without understanding the particular life of the communities from which they spring. It is within such a community that each of us works out his ideas of belief and unbelief. In certain communities, the probabilities of one decision or the other are especially high or especially low. For one chooses according as one sees; but one sees—probably—according as one has grown accustomed to see.

Many a young person in the United States today seems to be quite confused by the opposite attractions he feels in his intelligence and heart. It is taken for granted in most intellectual circles that an intelligent person does not believe in God, and certainly not in any institutional religion. Given the general panorama of belief in God in America and the life of institutional religion in America, the young person is inevitably attracted to unbelief. The story of many a sensitive, intelligent man's life—told often in our literature—appears to recapitulate the recent history of the West. Such a person moves from a pious childhood to a questioning and finally cynical adolescence; he moves from religion to enlightenment.

For in reaction against romantic, narrow, and anti-intellectual forms of religion, many of the best minds in the West have long since cut off their adherence to a communal religious faith and an intelligent belief in God. They devote their moral energy to this world. From "St. David" Hume, who bore witness to the possibility of living a life of moral goodness and equanimity without God, to Albert Camus, who was himself a secular saint, such men have created a new way of life. For the first time in human history, they have made unbelief a chosen project of the human will, and on a large scale.[2]

Nevertheless, in our day there is a "crisis of unbelief," just as there was once a "crisis of belief."[3] As events have come full circle, men on both sides seem more understanding of one another; perhaps each feels the shadow of the other in his heart. Many hundreds of thousands of young Americans, for example, have grown up in households that have been not religious but enlightened. Unprejudiced by an anti-intellectual religious upbringing, some are raising again the religious questions. They are not satisfied with their parents' view of life, but neither are they ready to return to the faraway religious life of their grandparents. They are torn by interior movements both of belief and unbelief, believing in a kind of God on Mondays, Wednesdays, and Fridays, and warning themselves against illusions, a failure of nerve, and intellectual cowardice on other days. They do not know which way to turn; their enlightenment has proved empty and fallacious, but the religious thought they encounter is unintelligent. Like the dry leaves of the *Inferno*, they blow back and forth in the empty spaces outside the gates of heaven and of hell.

Moreover, intellectual life in the United States is curiously cosmopolitan. To many uninitiated students, the European world of Camus and Sartre is at first strange and much too emotive. America did not truly know the terrors of this century's wars, neither the nihilism of the cafés nor that more terrible nihilism of the concentration camps. Americans did not see the values, traditions, and beliefs of the Middle Ages—so long, and necessarily, eroded—come crashing down in the flames of Berlin in 1945. A new world was about to arise in Europe; but no one exactly saw its shape.[4] Albert Camus wrote in *The Rebel*: "We are now at the extremities. At the end of this tunnel of darkness, however, there is inevitably a light, which we already divine and for which we have only to fight to ensure its coming. All of us, among the ruins, are preparing a renaissance beyond the limits of nihilism."[5]

Separated by an ocean from the nightmare of the Second World War, and by its too-short history from a sense of tragedy and sin, America has known neither the nihilism nor the need for renaissance. Philosophers, psychologists, social scientists, and engineers have maintained most of the optimism of the Enlightenment; there are countless millions of what Reinhold Niebuhr[6] calls "the soft utopians": moderate, pragmatic, prosperous, free of metaphysical concern. In only a few places is the American intellectual scene deeply affected by the more rigorous logical and linguistic rejection of metaphysics common in English philosophical circles. But here social and psychological reformers have just as effectively cleansed themselves of "the metaphysical emotions." The irrelevance of religious concern is so accentuated in America that one hardly knows how to raise a question of belief or unbelief. Indifference to religion is the ordinary mark of the serious intellectual.

Furthermore, modern science and technology have now made it practical to dream of a better life for all men, if only the intelligent and the generous labor mightily to do everything that men can. Many of the most idealistic are too busy for religion, a religion, moreover, which still speaks as if the world were agricultural and as if science, technology, and sprawling, dirty, busy cities did not exist. The words used by religion—salvation, providence, personal sin, resignation, grace—mean almost nothing to those who are trying to make the earth more habitable for men. The effective, moving symbol of the new unity of men from all nations is not the World Council of Churches nor the Second Vatican Council but the Olympic games, or the international collaboration of scientists, or perhaps the United Nations. Religion is still worthy of a small section in a magazine or a special half-page in the daily newspaper; and many readers may be presumed to turn those pages without curiosity, or never to open to them.

In the century of John Locke, it was possible to take many theological propositions as "self-evident," and to assume that "any sane man" would make the "obvious" inference, from the existence and order of things in this world to their Maker. The direction of contemporary philosophical inquiries is different. The question no longer is, Are assertions about God *true?* Nowadays the question is, What can assertions about God possibly *mean?* The philosopher can no longer rely on cultural unanimity to validate an appeal to "self-evidence."[7] When he does give a moment of attention to the matter, the nonbeliever asks the believer, When you say "God," are you willing to point to any possible presence of God in our experience? And, if not, how does your God who cannot be detected, and who makes no difference in our experience, differ from no God at all?

Many men would probably agree that an accurate image of human life is the ship of Theseus.[8] The ocean is unknown and featureless, and the task of science is pragmatic: to keep the ship afloat from day to day, replacing plank after plank as required, to make the ship more comfortable and safe as long as possible against the waves. There is no use attending to the night, for there are no stars, and there is no harbor. A man is well advised to turn his eyes from the rail, inward to the life on board. Let him make himself useful to the company, improve the ship, care for the needy, and enjoy himself. The sea is challenging, and even cruel; it is an adequate ship; its crew is partly noble, partly venal. Many are content.

Moreover, if the ordinary people of the world continue in large numbers to believe in God (although "the apostasy of the masses" is not a figure of speech, even where through custom many still go to church), it is not because their philosophers teach them that such belief is reasonable, or explain to them what such belief means. Generations ago, religious faith went one way in the West and intellectual life went another. A sizable number of professional philosophers, of course, still profess belief in God. But at present there hardly exists, even for them, a communicable philosophic language for expressing their belief in God and working out its problems. Moreover, far from gaining any philosophical advantage from their belief in God, such philosophers seem to inherit—so far as their nonbelieving peers are concerned—severe philosophical problems. The difficulty is that neither the nonbeliever nor the believer sees God; God remains hidden. The believer insists that his experience indicates to him that there is a God; that, though unseen, God is present in the world. The nonbeliever, in the same darkness, finds no such indications; makes no such inference; is aware of no such presence. He not only asks the believer, What do you see that I don't? He also suspects that the believer sees nothing intelligible at all.

An old language about the world and old images for the world have passed away. Men no longer think as they once did. The Anglican bishop of Woolwich, John A. T. Robinson, has with considerable force come upon this point, and upon another as well: that a mythical, pre-Copernican language about "a God 'out there' . . . seated on a throne in the empyrean heaven overseeing an earth-centered universe" is not about the true God at all.[9] Bishop Robinson sees the urgent need of Christianity to demythologize its antiquated language, but he wishes to put a new one in its place. At least concerning his second point, the language to be used about God, he thus falls into the very mistake he has freshly uncovered. Thomas Merton has written: "I for one am perfectly at home with the idea that mythical and poetic statements about God are not adequate representations of Him, but I am also used to thinking that no conceptual knowledge of God is perfectly adequate, and therefore when I see the Bishop busy with 'framing new concepts' I would be inclined to say he still had not grasped the extent of the problem. His anguish should perhaps be greater and more existential than it actually is. He quotes Tillich and Bonhoeffer, he protests with them against 'conditioning the unconditional' and yet I cannot help feeling that his book is, more than anything else, a job of 'reconditioning.' "[10]

But the main point of Bishop Robinson is well taken. Neat conceptions of design and order in the world, a mythology of "above" and "below," "supernature" reified as a second story to the observable world, and naïve images of God and heaven, if maintained, must mean the demise of Christianity among men of intellectual integrity. Images from another era of intellectual and social history no longer apply to men of industry, to laborers in rows of tenements, to mechanics and engineers. If the Russian Institute of Atheism was embarrassed because the West was not shocked when Russian astronauts reported that they found no God in the heavens, still, the havoc wrought in the religious imagination (both of intellectuals and of the people) by the course of modern civilization has not yet been adequately recorded. The culture of an industrial society no longer supports reflexive beliefs that drew strength from the everyday idiom of a simpler time; and the pace of city life does not encourage that critical search for self-knowledge nor that joy in creation which lead to God. The traditional "religious" culture is slipping from our civilization like a useless skin, and a new language and a new culture is taking its place.

If one were to decide for belief or for unbelief merely on the question of cultural context, one would have to choose unbelief; the man in tune with our culture does not believe in God. Recognizing this, some Christians abandon the ancient cultural context of belief in order to attach themselves unequivocally to the modern cultural context. God is in the world, they say, and nowhere else. "So the more secular one is, the more one discards the trappings of religion, the more one is united with God-in-the-world."[11] At first, such a program seems faithful to the utter transcendence of God, who is beyond the limitations of any cultural context, and yet is served when we serve other men. It seems to fulfill the evangelical program: "Whatsoever you do for the least of my brethren, you do for me." Becoming all things to all men, one becomes godless to the godless, secular to the secular, pragmatic to the pragmatists, a social reformer to social reformers. But then, all of a sudden, it seems more economical not to be a believer at all. Why not be simply godless?

Yet something in the human spirit warns one that there is more than this. Being an historical creature, one ought to be in tune with one's culture in things not evil (one would not want to have been in tune with Hitler's Germany); one ought to share the best thoughts, the best aspirations of one's time. To worship God, one ought not to have to turn one's imagination, emotions, words, and thinking backward to the worldly forms of another age. And on the other hand, to have experienced the true God—or at least to have experienced that part of oneself that is capable of detecting the limits of human intelligence and of standing reflectively, speechlessly, before the transcendent— is to see that human life is not a priori closed in upon itself. The human intelligence may possibly be open, not closed, to the transcendent God. This possibility, once recognized, staggers the intelligence. Beside this possibility, if it is not fictive, the amenities of the secular outlook are unworthy of a human being. If one is to be faithful to conscience, one must investigate the possibility. One does so with care, with calm reflection upon alternatives.

"We feel," Ludwig Wittgenstein once wrote, "that even if all possible scientific questions be answered, the problems of life have still not been touched at all." This is the voice of the young Wittgenstein, and he adds: "Of course there is no question left, and just this is the answer. The solution of the problem of life is seen in the vanishing of this problem."[12] But in Wittgenstein, as in many men, the conflict between the huge night and the fragility of Theseus' ship refuses to be stilled. How did that ship come to be there, so self-contained? Norman Malcolm records in his memoir an experience that Wittgenstein described by saying: "*When I have it I wonder at the existence of the world. And I am then inclined to use such phrases as 'How extraordinary that anything should exist!'*"[13]

Thus the question of God is fought out in the dark reaches of the human subject, not in the clear areas where the objects of mathematics, physical science, or even of familiar ordinary language, live and move. It occurs in an area of discourse that we are hardly able to countenance alongside our official sciences; it occurs outside the languages we have so far chosen for our intellectual life. A philosophy of the human subject—the title we may give the area in which it occurs, a philosophy that has not yet been worked out—will have to be invented as a public discipline, maintaining empirical controls and scientific methods. Such a philosophy will make other demands on the philosopher than the philosophy of science or the philosophy of ordinary language. It represents the area of greatest risk in philosophic work. It is not a quest for certainty, but for understanding; and not for understanding in the abstract, but for understanding of oneself. It requires a language we are forced, by sustained wonder about ourselves and about the possibility that there may be a God, to create.

In his sometimes severe review of Robinson's *Honest to God*, Thomas Merton has written: "Yet in all fairness I must admit that I think that I discovered the meaning of Christian faith when I found out that the usual mythological and anthropomorphic picture of God was not the true God of Christians. That is to say that, radically, my experience was close to that which I think underlies Dr. Robinson's book: the direct and existential discovery of God beyond concepts and beyond myths, in His inexpressible reality. Whether one speaks of Him as *ens a se* and pure act (which are the notions that gave me a certain amount of light), or whether one accepts Tillich's idea of God as the 'pure ground of all being' (as Bishop Robinson does), the important thing is a spiritual awareness of the supreme reality of God."[14]

It is a plain fact that some persons have stood before what they take to be God. If this experience has sometimes been had by oneself, then even if language limps in expressing it, and even if from many respected points of view the experience itself is explained away in various fashions, still, one may find it very difficult to evade. In that case, honesty to oneself requires that one labor to find words and the conceptual apparatus for making as plain as possible what seems to be important about the experience. To undertake this task on the present philosophic scene is to break new ground. There is, to be sure, a tradition for speaking of such things.[15] But it is ancient and arcane; it requires a measure of historical research that few men are inclined to expend, and merely to repeat its deliverances on the current scene would not solve the problem of how to speak of one's experience, even for one's own benefit, in the language of one's historical culture.

As a consequence, the search for one's own identity, and for a reflective resolution of the problem of belief and unbelief, leads one into an almost unwalked land. One must undertake an essay in revisionary metaphysics,[16] proposing a point of view for approaching and a language for expressing experiences about which philosophers of today are relatively silent.

2. *Clarifications: Belief and Faith*

By now it should be clear that the problem with which we are preoccupied is not that of religious faith, viz., not that of whether to accept the covenant of Moses or the covenant of Jesus as a supernatural bond between man and God. It is not the problem of revealed religion at all. The problem facing us is that of philosophic belief. If by intelligence we cannot know whether there is a God; if, that is, a man has no way of defending himself with critical intelligence against illusory beliefs, then the edifice of revealed religion is—for us, at least—on shaky ground. Our insistent question is whether there is a way to the living God through the use of human intelligence, through reflection upon one's own experience and identity. To make this distinction clear we have chosen to use the word "belief" for our concern, and have regularly reserved the word "faith" for that religious faith which comes by grace, is salvific, and beyond man's resources. (The word "believer" remains ambiguous; but in nearly all cases it refers in this study to those who have a philosophical belief in God.)

Perhaps it is a Catholic background that leads me to pose the problem in this way; perhaps. But after reflection I am driven back to the conviction that there is no other way of posing it when one is torn between belief and unbelief, or if one enters into dialogue with a friend who does not believe. When that cord is cut which attaches religious faith to the earthiness of man's intelligence, then religious faith is made to replace man's intelligence. And if a man without religious faith is thought to be unable to discover at least that there is a God, religious faith itself suffers two defeats. When philosophy and faith are allowed to go their separate ways, there is a defeat for the person of religious faith, because then he is in fact divided against himself, even if (under the shield of a "religious" culture) he does not notice the division. And there is a defeat for the community of religious faith, since such a faith cannot endure through cultural change without a philosophical, nonimaginative understanding of its own language and beliefs.

The complexity of human consciousness is such that a man seldom sees the contradictions latent in many of the things he believes, and often is able to live comfortably and complacently even while the pillars of his soul are being silently eroded. Even the believing community may not at first notice the contradictions it has allowed between its philosophy and its faith. The inherited faith may be so strong that philosophic countermoves may not take effect in the practical living and thinking of their originators. But the children of these originators will have to choose at some clearer parting of the ways—or their children's children. The abandonment of faith by British empiricists has since Locke proceeded in just this way. In the short run, faith without philosophy suffices. But for the community, and in the long run, intelligence will have its due.

I am well aware that some believers, chiefly Protestant Christians like Barth and existentialist Catholics, insist that philosophy and faith are such separate matters that philosophical belief is irrelevant to religious faith. Radical contradiction between philosophy and faith, they might say, does not give prima facie evidence of a deficiency either in philosophy or in faith. It points rather to the insufficiency of human intelligence, which is radically incapable of reaching God. Such believers are troubled by the pretensions of conceptualistic and rationalistic philosophy; they see clearly the defects of those seekers after the Absolute who end by making the Absolute subject to man's mind. The

God of Abraham, Isaac, and Jacob, they will say with Pascal (who was preoccupied with an early form of modern philosophical belief), is not the God of the philosophers.

In one sense, this type of Christian thinker stands near the nonbeliever. Neither such a Christian nor the nonbeliever finds a philosophy that reaches God, nor hopes for one. In another sense, he is at the opposite extreme from the nonbeliever. The latter puts all his trust in a philosophy inefficacious for finding God; the former puts his ultimate trust in a leap into God's grace. Such Christians I do not wish to imitate, although their motives win my sympathy and I feel closer to them by far than to conceptualists or rationalists. They are led, I believe, to a two-world theory of faith and intelligence in an effort to preserve faith from two vices. They wish to avoid a notional, conceptualistic theistic philosophy which is idolatrous in effect if not in intent; and to escape the closed world of the antitranscendent, atheistic philosophical programs of recent generations.

Such a division leaves the believer in a very weak intellectual position. Without a resolution of several severe philosophical problems, the philosophically trained mind cannot help being repelled by Jewish or Christian faith, and the faith of believers cannot be integrated with their philosophy. The nonbeliever justly refuses to commit himself to religious faith until he sees to what he is committing himself: what religious assertions mean. Given the current lack of a philosophic language for answering his questions, the nonbeliever feels that his nonbelief is a necessary economy. By the canon of parsimony, if he can do philosophy without the noumenal and live without grace, he must prefer the Spartan universe which has no God. The believer may accuse him of failing to note certain segments of human experience; but the nonbeliever will ask him, Which? The religious man, therefore, who decides that what counts in religious faith is commitment, a leap, the experience of encounter, who decides that the problems of philosophical belief may safely be overlooked, is at a grave intellectual disadvantage. He cannot say what he means by "God," or why he believes in God. Moreover, it is doubtful whether he can understand the relationship between his faith and the rest of his intellectual life. He is obliged to live as an intellectually divided man, in two worlds at once.

Apart from men of sophistication, like Barth, there is the simpler Christian fundamentalist, who seeks refuge from philosophy by repeating the words of the Scriptures or of his Church's doctrines. "It is better to feel compunction," the tradition of piety counsels him, "than to know how to define it." It is true, as Jacques Maritain once observed, that from a Christian point of view we shall finally be judged, not by how much we know, but by how much we have loved. But the very core of love is wisdom, discrimination, insight; blind love, as the corruption of the best is worst, wreaks a worse kind of harm than any other abuse, since against it there is no appeal. So likewise with the blind faith of the fundamentalist. Abandoning intelligence, he abandons all hope for an appeal to human integrity. Moreover, there is no need for a believer to be anti-intellectual; it is possible to be simple and yet not despise intelligence. A man of simple faith may want for words and be easily confused by questions; yet he need lack neither integrity nor insight. Long companionship with a simple man will often reveal the depths of his wisdom, which he nevertheless cannot articulate or defend. The fundamentalist commits a grave and unnecessary error in his polemic against intelligence; moreover, in the long run he will rue the loss of its support.

There is for the Christian, in short, no effective escape from philosophy. If he says that Christ is the firstborn of the Father, he is using a metaphor that seems familiar and limpid. No doubt the childlike mind takes up the point, neglecting the aspects that do not apply; children move without effort between image and reality. But as soon as the growing mind begins to question the metaphor, it finds itself searching for ever clearer philosophic terms, or at least for a principle of interpretation. The relationship between Christ and the Father is not literally that of a human son to a human father; biological generation is not in question. What kind of relationship is it then? The Father is eternal, but Christ is in history. What is eternity, what is the temporal order, and how can the two be related? The mind need not, and the contemporary mind generally does not, question the truth of such Christian doctrines; it asks the more radical question, What can they mean?

Similar problems—not specifically Christian—arise when one tries to say that God is good, or merciful, or the creator, or any of a dozen theological terms. Not every philosophy can make sense of the application of predicates from human experience to God. Some philosophers ask whether religious men are speaking fictively, elaborating a symbolic construction whose roots lie in their own imagination, fears, or desires. They ask if God is not like a gardener who, said to come to tend the garden late at night, is never detected by guards, watchdogs, or electric fence, and seems therefore indistinguishable from no gardener at all.[17] Unless the Christian who is a philosopher can explain, at least to himself, how these predicates are used of God, how can he assure *himself* that he is not talking about nothing at all, in a void peopled by his own imaginings? And of course, unless he little by little works out the philosophic tools for doing so, and for communicating his methods to other philosophers, the nonbeliever will be utterly unable to follow his use of language. The believer will live in two intellectual worlds, that of faith and that of philosophy, and so will the larger cultural community.

Unlike intellectual inquiry, however, action is singleminded, and thus it will happen in the world of work and action that faith will become increasingly irrelevant. Correspondingly, even the inarticulate but deep understanding of faith once operative in the culture will begin to wane. Men will find it next to impossible to understand the meaning of religious terms, either from philosophy or from habitual, inarticulate familiarity. Western culture is clearly in the throes of such a development. It is no wonder that the nonbeliever cannot understand the meaning of religious assertions. In many cases the believer has forgotten the meaning as well.

Some Christian writers, it appears, are struck so forcibly by the image of a "post-religious" age because they did not recognize the extent of the philosophical capital on which Western Christianity for centuries drew so heavily, but which is now exhausted. They are increasingly willing to recognize, however, that the natural soil of human life cannot yield fruit until it is thoroughly worked and made fertile by the tears and blood of believing intelligence. Busy men (themselves included) simply will not *attend* to what is unintelligible to them.[18] It is not enough, either for the individual or for the community of believers, to wait for God to rain down his grace. It is not enough for believers to go on merely "believing," not knowing why they believe, not attending to language, philosophy, and culture, unable to express the faith that is in them, absenting themselves from intellectual discussion. Men cannot listen long to the language of a foreign age, nor can even the man of faith long endure a life divided between two cultural worlds: he will give up one or the other.

In our generation, the gap between believers and nonbelievers has stretched to a terrifying width. Believer and nonbeliever sometimes appear to be like two different species of men, unable even to begin to speak to each other on an issue fundamental to both; they each think the other faintly mad. This situation is intolerable, if only because each man feels in his own heart impulses both of belief and of unbelief. Each man is an intelligent subject. Each seeks his own identity, and senses intimations (which he knows may be illusions) of the hidden God.

The individual inquirer is further rent, meanwhile, by those philosophical categories that divide the cognitive from the emotive, the objective from the subjective, reason from the heart, and thus misrepresent the realities of everyday experience. This is why reflection on these realities holds so much promise for a philosophical renewal and for the creation of a philosophical vocabulary with which to speak sensibly about the decision for belief or unbelief. Without such a vocabulary, religious faith is ultimately dumb, gagged by its own abdication of philosophical inquiry.

There are, however, serious objections against the line of inquiry we have been driven to undertake. Is not the man of faith denuded of his best vestiture if he begins to speak solely about philosophical belief? Does he not leave behind him everything of value he has to say? In truth, the man of faith who tries to speak a merely philosophical language cannot say everything he would wish to say, cannot exhaust his insight and his hope. It is also true that he runs the risk of speaking exactly like the nonbeliever, with no special contribution of his own. So long as he is on the nonbeliever's ground, the nonbeliever gives a wary assent; but as soon as he comes to speak of the richness and substance of his concrete religious experience, the nonbeliever is inclined to say: "Preposterous!"

Moreover, the man of faith who tries to philosophize may be so entrapped in the traditional definitions and logic of what used to be called "philosophical theology" that he will have lost the taste for God, the living experience, which makes inquiry real. He will so rationalize and conceptualize his faith that the detached observer will wonder whether he has ever truly known the living God, or only the formulae of books and relationships among words. I do not wish to score an easy victory by chastising a school of thought already maligned far beyond its deserts, but I have suffered through enough modern scholastic textbooks and lectures to recognize that this vice is the scourge of a scholasticism too much given to imitation, too little given to originality.

In such a system at its worst, the individual inquirer is too easily depersonalized, and authenticity has too little room to breathe. I can note with honesty and satisfaction that such works as those of Pieper,[19] Chenu,[20] Hoenen,[21] and many others[22] should speedily renew that tradition and lead it to the originality and power of which it is capable.

If he works within another tradition, however, the man of faith become philosopher can succumb to the eros of the Absolute and the perils of Germanic ontology. When one conceives of reason as the faculty of intuiting permanent structures in reality, conceptualizing these structures schematically, and ordering them logically in a monistic system, what one gains in neatness and rational pleasure one loses elsewhere: in history, contingency, variety, and individuality. In such a system—once one shakes one's head and breaks the spell—one recognizes a hubris as injurious to the empirical temper as to the historical, contingent Christian and Jewish faith.

Perhaps, then, apologists like Reinhold Niebuhr and T. S. Eliot,[23] who speak from the perspective of a biblical faith "in the round," are more to be emulated. Niebuhr truly resists ontology; to get around it, he speaks of man's "spirit" as against man's "nature,"[24] of the ability of the self to "transcend" itself and be free of "its nature" and "reason"[25] in order to cry out to the absolute. In his early writings, he tried to show how a biblical faith illuminated various recurrent patterns of social history; in his later writings, he has concentrated instead upon an introspective analysis of the self.[26] He notes that biblical faith sheds needed light upon basic human experiences: "The mysteries of good and evil in man's collective life"; the "individual experiences of sin and death, on the one hand, and of grace on the other hand"; "the capacity of the self to transcend not only the processes of nature but the operations of its own reason, and to stand, as it were, above the structures and coherences of the world"; "man's uneasy conscience"; "man's freedom, responsi-

bility, and sin"; "the grace which makes the freedom tolerable
and which overcomes the sin."[27]

Such an argument, in effect, suggests that the perplexed take
up "a point of view," accept faith as their "presupposition," and
then note how such presuppositions, like new spectacles, clarify
their experience. No set of presuppositions, it is stressed, is
rationally compelling. But the biblical viewpoint illuminates man's
history and nature better than any other. Such an argument will,
it is hoped, "dispose" the inquirer to hear the Word of God,
when and if it is addressed to him as it has been to no other, by
God's gracious and overflooding gift. Such an inquiry no doubt
has its point; yet it leaves one radically unsatisfied at certain
basic points. Perhaps one would feel no need for "reconciliation"
if one had not been nurtured within a Christian community. Perhaps one would think of the opening to the transcendent as
merely an illusion, which needs dispelling as one might dispel any
romantic dream. Perhaps the "presuppositions" of biblical faith
illuminate the experience only of those nourished in a biblical
community, in which feelings of helplessness, reconciliation, and
transcendence are learned from birth. It is quite certain that
Protestants describe them in words different from those used by
Catholics. Many persons one meets do not seem to share them,
nor even to regret their absence.

Thus I do not see how the radical inquiry can be anything but
philosophical. Naturally, one cannot begin anything without
presuppositions; but one may collect alternative sets of presuppositions, compare them, and criticize them—and one can do this
without limit, as long as one's intellectual energy and adapt-
ability hold out. If in order to choose among three sets of presuppositions one needs a fourth set from which to judge them,
one can also find a fifth set (or one of the earlier three) by which
to judge the fourth. There is no such thing as a "pure" position.
But the human mind does not seem to be permanently confined
to the patterns of its earlier conditioning; self-criticism develops,

conversions occur, and patterns of intellectual behavior are amenable to argument among those whose minds are not decisively closed.

Belief in God does not go nearly so far as religious faith. The God of philosophy remains hidden, and does not reveal himself. To philosophers qua philosophers, he does not speak as he did to Abraham, Isaac, and Jacob. From philosophical inquiry one hopes to learn merely whether there are reasons for deciding that there is a God, and to formulate adequate criteria for defending oneself against false gods and illusions. It is the living God one seeks, though through philosophic inquiry one does not hope to see him. One hopes to be able to discover a method for deciding intelligently whether or not there is a God; and as the content of this decision is different from any other, so the method may also be. A philosopher therefore does not demand that this question behave like all other questions. He only demands that it be tractable by a method that commends itself to his critical intelligence. A philosopher hopes other men will concur in his method and good judgment. But in the end he hopes to be honest most of all to himself.

It is also possible that he will decide that there is a God, but will find it impossible to conceptualize what God is like, and will then go on to decide that Judaism and Christianity are seriously in error. It is possible to believe in God without having religious faith. The question before each of us is whether he has reasons for deciding that belief in God, or unbelief, is the more intelligent conclusion from his experience; and whether belief or unbelief better dissipates the darkness in which his identity lies hid. In the eyes of religious faith perhaps no man is saved or justified by the kind of belief we are seeking. No matter. It is the integrity of our conscience that leads us to seek it. If such a belief is possible, religious faith—should God speak—remains a possibility open to intellectual conscience. If such a belief is not possible, religious faith demands in effect that a man go down on all fours, humbled in the very intelligence and freedom to decide knowingly which constitute his dignity. Religious faith will seem to be a betrayal of man's own self.

"You must lose yourself to find yourself," the man of religious faith may say. "But there are many ways of losing oneself," the nonbeliever will say; "and the only way to defend myself against some of them is to scrutinize all of them with critical intelligence. Take intelligence from me and what would I have to offer to your God, presuming that there is one?"

2 ❖

PHILOSOPHY

AS SELF-KNOWLEDGE

1. In the Beginning Comes Decision

Nevertheless, the difficulty for a man born into a tradition of religious faith—which at times makes such eminent sense out of his experience—is that philosophical accounts of belief in God so little match his experience and so poorly express his point of view. It is not that the technicalities of philosophic discourse, the distinctions and counterdistinctions, offend his religious sense; both theology and religious tradition elaborate comparable signs of technical sophistication. It is rather that descriptions of religious phenomena given by philosophers rarely seem to be describing his own experience of religion. Or again, that conceptions which he finds quite inadequate are attributed to believers. Or again, that distinctions are not made between certain believers and some others, between scholars and ordinary believers, between Baptists and Lutherans, between philosophically inclined Catholics and scripturally inclined Catholics. When he hears nonbelievers speak of religion it is a little like hearing Eskimos describe trees, grass, and flowers.

It is correspondingly so difficult to speak of religion in many contemporary philosophical contexts that many believers are tempted to give up argument with some philosophers and to write off certain kinds of philosophy as simply irrelevant to their experiences and concerns. I have several times heard distinguished religious thinkers refer to the complacent inattention and barely disguised hostility they have been treated to on the occasion of public "dialogue" between religious thinkers and nonbelieving philosophers; the philosophers in turn express their own dissatisfaction with the "muddied" or "clear but false" reasoning of the religious thinkers. Are the two worlds necessarily so divided? Are intelligent men of goodwill so fundamentally different?

It is only with temerity, and not much hope of success, that one enters into the no-man's-land between them. But how can one live with oneself if one does not try? And, perhaps, where one man fails another will do better.

There is an area of philosophical inquiry, as we have earlier suggested, where the heart of the decision between belief and unbelief seems to lie. And the reason for difficulties in communication between believers and nonbelievers may be that we do not know very much about this region: the structure and requirements of intelligent subjectivity. For it is by intelligent subjectivity that one chooses a world view, or a life policy, or even to take this concrete line of action rather than that other equally plausible line; at least it is so when we "know what we are doing."[1] Intelligent subjectivity is a great, indefinite region in our intellectual and our active life, like a silent snow-covered hollow virtually untrod upon.

Thus, reflection upon the decision between atheism and theism leads one toward the center of one's self. Does theism or atheism lead me to what I am? Which offers the fruitful focal point by which to direct my understanding and my living? Which establishes my autonomy? Which is a myth, and which reality?

John Courtney Murray thinks that the *old* "modern" problem of God concerned arguments about God's essence and existence, about God as a principle of explanation; the problem today, he argues, is different. The "post-modern" problem lies, he believes, "in the historical-existential order." The terms of the argument are God's presence or God's absence.[2] Post-modern men "have said that God is dead. So the affirmations clash. For believers say that God is living." The issue is whether the myth or the reality is "in Sartre of Paris or in Paul of Tarsus."[3] Not explanation but experience is at stake; not logic but a way of life. But, as Father Murray also notes,[4] America is still living in the "modern" age: the main reason for denying that there is a God is that neither science nor the marketplace nor the political life of the city seems to have need of him; as a principle of explanation, the idea of God is useless. The thesis of intellectual life in America is that there is no God. A man seems foolish to dissent.

The only way to answer the radical question is to search one's heart. What is at stake is a decision: to decide to root one's life in God's life, or in one's own. Which is more intelligent? One cannot choose to do both; and the identity one has inherited may be mistaken. In reflection one must ask oneself, Who am I? Seeking to decide whether there is a God, one is led to that love of wisdom which is—or used to be—philosophy.

Philosophy is the science of self-knowledge. But the outcome of any philosophical inquiry is determined by its starting place. The conception of philosophic method chosen in the beginning governs the conclusions at the end. The key focus for fruitful philosophical inquiry does not concern conclusions, nor even premises, nor even the connections between conclusions and premises. It concerns the question of "horizon."[5] A horizon is the limit of what can be seen from a determinate point of view; it has a subjective and objective pole; it relates the subject to the range of matters which he can investigate from that viewpoint. A philosopher rises or falls by how critical he is of his own starting place, and how broad his knowledge is of alternative points of view. Each conception of philosophic method has its advantages and disadvantages. What is crucial to a philosopher seems to be not so much what he can work out within his own horizon, but how capable he is of sharing other horizons and justifying the choice he has made of his own.

The primary emphasis in the discipline of philosophy, therefore, does not fall upon logical relationships between propositions, or the defining and establishing of terms. The enunciation of a system of propositions is at best secondary to philosophy. The primary task of the philosopher is to reflect upon his own horizon, his purposes, the tools he has been taught by his teachers, and the tools available in other philosophical traditions. The primary imperative in philosophy is not *Construct a consistent system*. The primary imperative is *Know thyself*.

Philosophy has many tasks: to examine the structure and methods of the arguments of the sciences, for example, and to study the workings of ordinary language. But when it neglects the imperative that would lead each philosopher to self-knowledge —and to a certain intellectual humility—the very center of the enterprise is neglected. Then, like an apple devitalized by a worm, its shiny surface too begins to wrinkle, and the season of philosophy seems to have passed. Any "revolution" or "renewal" in philosophic history is not yet complete that has not raised questions of self-knowledge. Moreover, acute discomfort will be felt about the prospects of such a renewal, even by their proponents. Gilbert Ryle, for example, concluded his "manifesto of analytic philosophy" with a certain sorrow that his starting place involved him in the eventual evacuation of philosophy; although he did not, at the time, question that starting place.[6]

The need for both theoretical and concrete attention to self-knowledge is apparent also among those philosophers most concerned with such impersonal, systematic disciplines as mathematics and physics. They must assume a certain view on what it is to know, and a certain concept of the human person. Moreover, they take this view of knowing strictly, and bend every effort to train novices to its rigors. They insist on the study of logic and language, a recondite and demanding discipline, often extremely abstract and (in a certain sense) "objective." Their concern for human history may be minimal, and their approach to problems quite nonhistorical. But even though they make such demands upon the human person, and even though they are themselves often companionable men of highly developed reflective judgment, their chief theoretical emphasis may fall upon the grammar, postulates, propositions, and laws of inference that professionally preoccupy them. They may not give as much theoretical attention to the horizon—viewpoints, outlooks, and directions—they have personally appropriated, according to which they live (or blame themselves if they do not), and by which they have become the kinds of persons, and even philosophers, they are. Their primary interest may lie with logical system, not with horizon; with words, not with themselves or others.

This option, of course, is open to those who can give good reason for wishing to imitate them, just as other options have been followed, with good or bad reasons, in other seasons of philosophy. Such options define a philosophical movement; decisions are the root of philosophy. A philosopher decides what he thinks human knowing is, and thus defines a vision of man, man's aims, and the attitudes fruitful for man to take. There are, moreover, many hypotheses about what it is to know, although the activity of knowing is readily accessible to each philosopher who proposes one of the hypotheses. The variety of hypotheses forces the student to conclude either that men experience knowing differently or that (though the experience is the same for all) it is an experience exceedingly difficult to articulate in a fashion that satisfies all.

Approaches to philosophy seem to differ primarily because of their differing articulations of the activity of knowing. The radical question to be asked of each philosopher is, "How do you know that you know?" When Hume says that what we know is solely our own impressions or logical relationships, or when A. J. Ayer in *Language, Truth and Logic*[7] says that the only meaningful assertions are tautologies or else propositions testable in sense experience, we have our hands on the dynamic core of their system, and need only watch it unfold from there. When Kant divides synthetic judgments from analytic, and describes the distinction between a priori and a posteriori, the dynamics of his extraordinarily arduous system are poised in anticipation, and we may sketch in, as if with dotted lines, the course of development they will have to take.

This point can scarcely be stressed sufficiently. There are many schools of philosophy; each has its own hypothesis concerning human knowing. In each school this hypothesis is the most fundamental, the most radical, the most determinative hypothesis. For in his doctrine about knowing, the philosopher establishes the methods, criteria, rules for argument, discovery, relevance, and evidence by which his philosophy will conduct itself on each question submitted to it. In his doctrine of knowing, he defines himself and his own view of the world. His hypothesis about knowing determines the outcome of his every other notion. This hypothesis is like a Midas' touch: it turns everything it touches its own coloring.

But to decide upon a doctrine of knowing is to have resolved the problem of one's own identity. It is a mistake to think that materialism or idealism or any other view of life is a conclusion to philosophic reasoning; it is rather a horizon already determined by the starting place, the point at which one has decided (or merely happened) to begin. Whatever one takes knowing to be determines what one will be able to know. Whatever it is in oneself that one trusts determines what one will think one's knowing to be. A materialist is already a materialist in his view of himself, before he has articulated his doctrine of knowing and his doctrines about the known.

Philosophy begins with a decision about oneself. Such a decision may or may not be responsible; a man may have inherited it or simply drifted into it. But it can be made responsibly, since it is subject to criticism and one can to some extent give an account of it. Moreover, different men can compare their different decisions and different accounts. In this way, the radical decision is suffused with intelligence; it is radical but not blind. On the other hand, the danger of radical irresponsibility is greater where the tide of public opinion flows in one's own favor. In the eighteenth century, belief in God was the conventional wisdom and the easier course; today, atheism is more or less taken for granted, and belief is suspect.

To believe today that scientific method is the key to man's identity is in some intellectual circles a highly honored belief; it would be so in all, no doubt, if there were some agreement about what constitutes scientific method, particularly in different fields of inquiry. But when one's conception of scientific method is limited by the uses of that method in physics and mathematics, then one's view of man is likely to be a little strange to men who have other conceptions. For the laws of mathematics and physics seem mainly to regard the impersonal rather than the personal, the species or class rather than the individual, the general rather than the singular.

Men alert to the contingencies of history fear the dictatorship of the automated brain, which has become, perhaps, the symbol of their hesitations about science as a way of life. Perhaps it is only that they are not yet accustomed to the power and promise of the new mechanical monsters, and that so far such prodigies of mathematics and physics are relatively primitive and gross. The contingencies, surprises, and approximations that men have come to recognize as familiar in everyday life, and which they do not wish to surrender to a mechanical brain, may at some later date be predicted more delicately—at least as delicately as by the most clairvoyant, political, and concrete human mind. But if it does happen that mathematical and physical methods of sufficient complexity will allow us to deal better than we do now with the contingent, the particular, the singular choices of historical action, will our conception of mathematics and physics have been changed in the process? The key lies in the phrase "sufficient complexity." Men are not so afraid of science as of scientism; they fear intellectual insensitivity, a lack of respect for all the rough edges, angles, and idiosyncrasies of human life as they have come to know it. They fear a ruthless justice that has no grasp of the organic, the fragile, and the singular factors of human history.

But, in any case, philosophy begins with a decision. To decide who I am is to decide what I think knowing is. And to decide what I think knowing is, is to determine the content and the limits of what I will know. Could I understand my understanding correctly, I could understand myself. Understanding myself, I would be prepared to live with other men, among things, without being at cross-purposes with myself.[8] So to understand my understanding and to treat others, things, and myself according to the demands of understanding would seem to be to live as well as a man might. To live such a life is to establish the most fruitful context for inquiring about God; in some other contexts, the question cannot even arise, and in others the answer to it is foreclosed.

2. Types of Self-knowledge

Since philosophy begins with a decision, it may properly be viewed as an invitation to a conversion of life. To begin to live philosophically is to begin to live an examined life, to be able to account for one's radical decision. The philosopher is one who is reflective, concerned with understanding what constitutes knowing in one kind of situation, and how to relate that knowing to knowing in another kind of situation. He seeks unity, not so much among propositions in a logical system (though that too) as among his diverse activities as a human person. A man who knows something, and knows to what degree he knows it, because he knows what it is for him to know, has made progress in gaining conscious possession of himself; he is skilled in the matter of philosophy. This is why philosophy belongs to all men. The professional philosopher studies the alternatives in more detail, at more length, than the ordinary man has time to do. But the professional philosopher, as an occupational hazard, is tempted to betray his own discipline by making primary what is secondary, by becoming not a more self-possessed and profounder person but a builder of systems. Philosophy is more fully conscious living; it is not like cataloguing butterflies, nor like a game of tinker-toys with words. The philosopher's empire is his own inner life; it is there that he is king—a humble king if he shares the wisdom he professes to love.

On the other hand, the self-knowledge of the philosopher is not like that encouraged by the moralist. Philosophy is more inclusive than ethics. The philosopher is not only interested in "living morally" according to some justifiable code or other. He is also interested in the relation between his scientific knowledge and his ethical judgments, between his religious, aesthetic, and moral sense and his everyday experience. The moralist may be interested in the qualities of moral action; the philosopher is interested in all the experiences and abilities of the human person. The philosopher can afford not to be a moralist, and still act as well—even by the moralist's standards—as the moralist. For the philosopher will have striven to act exactly as he reflects: with integrity, faithful to himself and to all factors in the situation. A moralist who is not also a philosopher may have a narrow approach to moral action, since his view may be confined to the moral code he defends. He often fixes on a rule of thumb or a pattern of conformity, which may or may not be enough to do justice either to the person acting or to the demands of the concrete situation. When such a moralist speaks of self-knowledge, he means that according to a certain code men should beware of rationalization and be honest about their motives. The philosopher means that a man should know the range of his abilities as a man.

Nor, in the second place, is philosophy to be confused with empirical psychology. The science of psychology is the study of behavior; it treats men as things; it observes men as objects. Such a study is highly useful; it is an instrument of prediction and control, for the individual and for society. It is useful because the data of moral experience are located by each man in the whole stream of his experience. As Aristotle remarks, unless a man is in his youth taught to feel correctly pleasures and pains, and shame and pride, he will not even have the data for correct moral judgment of the noble and the ignoble; he will never have tasted the one, nor have been taught to recognize the other.[9] Thus, scientific knowledge about the effects of various kinds of conditioning is crucial to political society. It is especially important to those political societies that wish to further the development of as many independent, critical, creative persons as they can. It is relatively easy to condition for conformity; to condition for freedom is far trickier.

But the science of psychology, in our age at least, has not yet resolved a certain equivocation in its conception and use of scientific method. For example, B. F. Skinner in his small classic, *Science and Human Behavior*, alternates between thinking of science as "first of all a set of attitudes"; and, on the other hand, "a search for order, for uniformities, for lawful relations among events in nature."[10] These two emphases, of which Skinner favors the second, relate science first to the person who has it, and second to the impersonally treated uniformities, laws, and relations that are its objects. There is in Skinner a systematic ambiguity concerning these contrary directions, personal and impersonal, in which science faces. It is clear that for the continuance and progress of science, individual human *persons* must develop the requisite skills and attitudes. Among these are, for example, the commitment to professional honesty, habits of technical care, the creative observance of methodological principles. Science, therefore, depends on the personal commitment of many young people, and their fidelity throughout life. Moreover, science may be presumed to have a serious effect on their nonprofessional attitudes, emotions, and ways of life. The pursuit of science, therefore, demands a high price of the human person. A scientist in love, a scientist in politics, may or may not be an adequately prepared human being. Thus, the scientist too must return to the self-knowledge enjoined by Socrates, and must judge himself in the light of what he decides it is to be a man. He must learn how to relate his professional knowing to other kinds of human knowing, and to other human activities.

In our generation it is easy to be preoccupied with the impersonal aspects of science and to neglect the human person. In the first place, the sciences prospered when they gave up "psychologism": reliance on intuition, insight, hunch, self-evidence, or other introspective criteria of truth. The science of psychology appeared to make swifter, surer strides once it abandoned the introspective methods of Wundt and the early pioneers in the field. Thus, theoreticians about scientific method, and practitioners who use it in the field are led to give more and more attention to "objective" factors, to events that can be publicly observed and publicly checked. On the other hand, with the systematic use of Occam's razor and of the canon of parsimony, scientists are ill-disposed to countenance any explanation that exceeds "objective" evidence. Thus, the scientist can hardly help thinking of himself as an observer, outside the experiment, looking on coolly, dispassionately, objectively, even though it has become clear that in certain types of experiments the action of the observer affects the result. Moreover, the emphasis on the public nature of his observation makes him, as a unique person, quite dispensable; anyone systematically trained and well-situated could do as well. Knowledge is power, Francis Bacon said; science is an instrument of prediction and control, Skinner writes. The more emphasis one puts on the impersonal, instrumental side of science, the more one makes the scientist an artisan, a dispensable cog in an onrolling machine. If science is merely pragmatic and instrumental, the scientist is valuable to society not for what he is but for what he does. He is more an object than a person.

On the other hand, the progress of science depends on the idiosyncrasies, original insights, extraordinary devotedness, and critical, independent nonconformity of at least a few persons. The relation between tradition and the individual talent is at least as complex in science as in literature or in religious faith. At present, psychologists like Skinner seem to be waging a necessary polemic against the traditions of scientific theory with which they are familiar: the introspection of the Continental idealist tradition, and the atomistic individualism of the British empiricists. Against the former, Skinner insists on public methods and objective controls; against the latter, he insists on the importance of the community, even for the individual talent. Both these moves lead him to overlook the personal elements, which poke their heads up through his theory at intervals, only to be submerged again. Skinner himself is a creative and critical thinker, a person and not only an object in the world and not only an observer "outside" it.[11] Not even his own polemical enthusiasm nor careful theory can prevent this side of him from showing. An interpretation of human knowing must account for this and other sorts of subjectivity.

If science is conceived to be a tool and its value is judged by its effectiveness in dealing with the world, it has no room for a concept of the human subject or the self. Skinner is bothered by this very point: "What is meant by the 'self' in self-control or self-knowledge? When a man jams his hands into his pockets to keep himself from biting his nails, *who* is controlling *whom*?"[12]

Skinner's conception of science is useful when there are two objects between which to establish a functional relation. But the self is not an object, and it cannot entirely be known in the manner of objects. A man who tries to observe his "self," whether by introspection or any other direct assault upon it, will not find it. Skinner tries to find a self by his methods and, like Hume, fails. "The self is most commonly used as a hypothetical cause of action. So long as external variables go unnoticed or are ignored, their function is assigned to an originating agent within the organism. If we cannot show what is responsibility for a man's behavior, we say that he himself is responsible for it. . . . The practice resolves our anxiety with respect to unexplained phenomena."[13] Very shortly, Skinner concludes: "A concept of self is not essential to an analysis of behavior . . ." and refers to such a concept as an "explanatory fiction." A few lines later he adds: "It appears that a self is simply a device for representing *a functionally unified system of responses.*"[14] He explains the functional unity of such systems without a concept of a self.

This point marks the crucial difference between scientific psychology, as now conceived, and philosophy. Scientific psychology, even in systems not like Skinner's, appears to favor the relationship of observer and objects; even the introspective psychologist seems to "look inside" himself and claim to observe there certain objects or events. But in Skinner's system the difference is especially clear. Skinner makes an object of the self, and then denies that such an object can be discovered. This is the central move in Skinner's book and the reason for his unresolved conflict between a personal and an impersonal view of science. As a tonic against the traditional individualism of English liberal philosophy, and against the idealist postulation of the self as a mysterious object beyond science, Skinner's analysis is therapeutic. As an analysis of the experience of the self, it is only partial. To express in theoretical terms the concrete experience of the self, one must avoid speaking of the self as if it were an object among other objects. When two friends converse and address one another as "I" and "you," they may replace neither form of address by "it" without doing violence to the experience of communication they share. They are not objects in confrontation. Philosophy is self-knowledge in the sense that it respects the fact that one's experience of oneself is *sui generis*. It does not try to understand one's experience of oneself according to the model of observer and object. Psychology tends to focus one's attention on others as objects; whereas philosophy instructs a man to attend to himself, and if to others, then as to persons.

The impact of persons on each other has hardly yet been studied. Feuerbach long ago wrote: "I reconcile myself, I become friendly with the world only through my fellow men. . . . A man existing absolutely alone would be lost without any sense of his individuality in the ocean of nature; he would neither comprehend himself as man, nor nature as nature."[15] Rarely does creative work prosper in an isolated individual, or even through the second-best stimulation of books. Men seem to discover their own personal identity only in communion with others. Painters usually flourish together; writers seek one another out; scientific conventions bring together, not papers and books, but living persons. Men seem to come to understand, to love, and to be inspired, through communion with other men; not through mere contiguity, but through communion. Faith comes by hearing; the ear is the chief sense of learning;[16] men seem to be created as persons in proportion as they communicate with each other through sensitive, sympathetic presence. Psychology attends to objects, philosophy to persons.

Thirdly, if the self-knowledge of philosophy is not to be confused with that of the moralist nor that of the psychologist, neither is it to be confused with that gained through psychotherapy. With or without the help of a psychiatrist, a man can come to increasing insight into those emotional patterns of his that were shaped by past experiences, and which well up unseen from his unconscious, only occasionally to appear as symbols in dream, in imagination, or in behavior. Such insight is unquestionably part of the injunction *Know thyself*. On the other hand, it is specialized. It is chiefly concerned with one's unconscious symbolic life. More generally, it is concerned with universal symbols and the wellsprings of the human activity of symbolizing. But man is more than his unconscious, and is capable of many other activities besides that of imaginative symbolization. The self-knowledge to which philosophy invites man is of the unity and the identity in all these activities, but primarily of man's conscious life. The philosopher seeks to understand that understanding by which he can become aware of elements of his unconscious life previously hidden from him, or of the symbols and actions issuing from his unconscious life.

Fourthly, if B. F. Skinner's choice of a view of man indicated one alternative among which we may choose, that of a philosophical pragmatist like Sidney Hook indicates another. Professor Hook takes a rather large and flexible view of scientific method. He follows Dewey and Russell in holding to the proposition *"All knowledge that men have is scientific knowledge."*[17] Or again: "It can be shown that all human beings in their everyday experience are guided by the conception of knowledge as scientific knowledge. To deny this is palpably insincere."[18] But to what are we committed if we affirm what we must then affirm? What Mr. Hook seems to mean by scientific knowledge centers around the notion of prediction: "There must be reasoned grounds for making one prediction about the future rather than another and confirmations greater than what one would expect on the basis of chance."[19] But Mr. Hook's understanding of man is already involved: "In short, the justification for asserting that all knowledge is scientific is not a matter of definition but is, rather, pragmatic: such a view enables us to achieve our ends in the world, whatever they are, more effectively."[20] But what are our ends in the world?

In an earlier chapter, Mr. Hook has made it plain that he takes "technological and practical behavior as the matrix of the reasonable."[21] He summarizes the naturalism to which he is committed: "The naturalist believes that his assumptions are reasonable because they express, in a more general way, no more than what is expressed by any non-philosopher as well as by all philosophers, whatever their school, in their successful working practice in solving problems concerning the nature of things."[22] By "successful" he means "something as simple, naïve, and indefeasible as discovering a substance that subjected to friction will burst into flame, building a house that will withstand an earthquake, producing a seed that will yield a better harvest."[23] Thus Mr. Hook's conception of successful knowledge seems to be phrased totally in terms of prediction and control. Again: "Naturalism, as a philosophy, is a systematic reflection upon, and elaboration of, the procedures man employs in the successful resolution of the problems and difficulties of human experience."[24] Mr. Hook, in short, appears to see himself as a technician; man is a solver of problems.

Thus Mr. Hook, rather broadly, makes scientific method identical with "the commitment to the processes and methods of critical intelligence."[25] Next, he confines this commitment to the world of common sense and pragmatic science. That is why he can speak of "success," "the resolution of problems," the ability "to achieve our ends in the world . . . more effectively." But the question at issue may be whether the worlds of common sense and science exhaust human abilities, needs, or interests. Does commitment to critical intelligence come to an end in keeping Theseus' ship afloat? Mr. Hook warns us that naturalism is a "proposal,"[26] a "decision,"[27] a "commitment."[28] He thereby teaches us the need for careful methods of self-knowledge, a gradual, conscious appropriation of our own intelligent subjectivity. The decision we ultimately make is "not arbitrary: one can give good reasons for it or point to the historical evidence that makes it a reasonable decision."[29] "Every conception of knowledge must make assumptions about what constitutes knowledge, and one such set of assumptions will be incompatible with another. . . . The question once more becomes: are our assumptions arbitrary or reasonable?"[30]

Prior to the world of common sense and scientific method, we may conclude, is the decision of the human subject concerning which experiences to admit as relevant, which data to count as evidence, in its understanding of itself and the world in which it is inserted. The human subject authenticates common sense and scientific method as suitable means to specified ends, in virtue of its own independent, reflective life. On Mr. Hook's testimony, the human subject accumulates reasons and scrutinizes its past experiences in order to justify this decision in its own presence. But are the rational needs of the self exhausted when it has dealt effectively with the problems of the object world? The self shows a certain independence in the justification it seeks for its reliance upon common sense and scientific method. The self thus raises questions that common sense and science do not answer. It passes judgment on common sense and science. Does the commitment to critical intelligence, one wonders, lead a man beyond naturalism, beyond the object world? If so, it would have to lead beyond naturalism not by "hunches, guesses, visions, revelations, *a priori* reasoning."[31] It would lead beyond naturalism by reflection on the data of intelligent subjectivity, on the contrasting proposals for interpreting it, and on the accumulating of reasons for accepting one interpretation rather than another.

Thus we may accept Hook's generic sense of scientific method, viz., the scrutiny of data in which to verify hypotheses. But we must extend the use of this generic method beyond the "technical and practical behavior" that Mr. Hook takes as "the matrix of the reasonable." The matrix of the reasonable is not bounded by the arena of pragmatic extroversion and the problems of the object world; it also includes the questions raised by intelligent subjectivity and the problems of man's origin and destiny. A generalized form of scientific method rules in this arena, too, but not according to the specific pragmatic, extroverted turn which Mr. Hook gives scientific method. A pragmatism that will account for intelligent subjectivity must be broader than his.

A wider view of pragmatism has been suggested by Morton V. White in his book *Toward Reunion in Philosophy*.[32] Professor White distinguishes between a hypothetical mechanical man who is simply wound up to make correct predictions, and the man who can account for his correct predictions. It is only the latter who qualifies as a scientist or even as a rational man; a principle for making correct predictions is not a sufficient criterion for science or for philosophy.[33] Professor White therefore attempts to broaden the meaning of pragmatism, in a move not unlike that of John Henry Newman, who tried to extend Aristotle's faculty of ethical judgment, *phronesis*, from ethics to other speculative concerns.[34] Professor White, following Nelson Goodman, argues that a "counterpart of conscience" is required to explain the decisions of philosophers and scientists.[35] The inquiring mind feels the bite of the normative, of a quasi-conscience. Philosophy, therefore, begins to recognize the operation of "pinned-down statements" that are normative, and that tell us which other statements we ought to accept and enroll among our approved beliefs.

At this point,[36] Professor White avoids the mistake of those who try to establish a changeless set of absolutes, apart from considerations of history and the real, by trying to spell out these "pinned-down statements" once and for all. He wisely opposes any attempt to simplify, or universalize them. He knows of no single absolute principle, no necessary and sufficient condition, by which these pinned-down statements are to be selected. Many such pinned-down or terminal criteria are needed; each is tentatively expressed and subject to criticism, reflection, and weighing in the balance against other terminal sentences. Professor White, in short, appears to be arguing for fidelity to what we shall later call the disinterested, unrestricted drive to understand. He urges: "The myth that we fix our stable points by peering at meanings, qualities, attributes, or propositions must be surrendered."[37] Instead, he gives his allegiance to critical reflection, "a process of resolving tensions and conflicts" among competing criteria. He admits the serious truth in pragmatism, but insists that pragmatism must be defined more broadly, more pluralistically, to include such other criteria as simplicity and "quasi-conscience." He concludes his book by hoping that philosophers, each from his own tradition and area of interests, will "once more realize that philosophy can be varied as life itself."[38]

But how are we to reach such criteria as those of White's "quasi-conscience" or of Newman's "illative sense"? How are we to justify any criteria to ourselves, except in becoming clear about our own identity as knowers? Every argument about deciding on the criteria by which to conduct one's inquiries and one's actions is of necessity circular: it begins from and returns to one's idea of one's self. To justify a theory about what knowing is, one must have a theory about the knower, i.e., the self. The circularity may be broken only at one point. In intelligent self-consciousness, a man may be able to criticize his justifications and his way of knowing, and try alternatives. As a knower, he has the requisite experience. His problem is to discover the most favorable disposition and the most fruitful attitudes for correct knowing, and tests by which to eliminate common sources of error. Richard B. Brandt's "qualified attitude method"[39] is one attempt to meet the problem. But to succeed in such an attempt, one must understand the dynamics of inquiry, both what drives inquiry along and what brings it to rest.

It seems necessary, in short, to come to terms with one's self. When I understand an argument, or see the point of a joke, or understand another man's character, what is it that I am doing? What are obstacles and what are aids to understanding? No one can decide whether or not he believes in God until he decides what his understanding is and can do. When he reaches that decision, he understands his limits and his possibilities. He may understand them correctly or incorrectly. If incorrectly, he will be alienated from himself. If correctly, he will have found himself.

3 ❖
DECIDING WHO I AM

1. Subject World and Object World

Philosophy, it then appears, requires a new kind of life.[1] A man takes possession of himself as a knower; he is different afterward from what he was before. He becomes reconciled to his limitations and determined to exploit his possibilities. A philosopher is one who professes to be faithful to his understanding of who he is, of what it is to be a man; and all men are, in part, philosophers. "To be faithful" to understanding, moreover, means to reject as often as possible the flight from understanding, both in inquiring and in acting; to try to expose one's own favorite self-deceptions, both in understanding and in doing. "To be faithful" is to *try*. No one quite succeeds. But some correct their mistakes more quickly than others, criticize themselves more ruthlessly, advance in honesty more constantly.

An assumption that seems plausible, and upon which our seeking after God may best be based, is that inquiry about God does not begin where inquiries into the functions or the natures of objects in the world begin. Inquiry about God begins with reflection upon the experiences proper to the human person, as a person. These experiences cannot be "observed." A man is made aware of their presence and their efficacy reflectively and indirectly. To analyze them one must allow them to emerge in consciousness. One must then advert to them; one must ponder them reflectively. This means that in pursuing God the inquirer's attention ought not to be a looking outward, as it is accustomed to be in dealing with objects in the world. It ought to be retrieved from the observation of objects or the making of hypotheses about them, and turned to reflecting about the inquirer himself: the observer and the maker of hypotheses. The beginning of the search for God lies in reflection upon oneself. The search for God is intimately connected with the discovery of one's own identity.

Moreover, to come to know oneself as a subject—as a person, as one who is conscious, who reflects, decides, and acts—is different from knowing oneself as an object. To know oneself as an object is, as it were, to take a position *outside* oneself—"on the ceiling"—and to watch oneself act, or think, or feel. It is to introspect. It is to be self-consciously conscious of self. It is to dissect, analyze, bargain with, and perhaps manipulate oneself. It is (at one limit) to set oneself upon the way to schizophrenia: the subject isolated, suppressed, and lost, yet somehow watching an object that it has made surrogate for itself.

It is also, of course, to think about the self, to make statements about it, and even to speak of the self as self, the subject as subject; in these ways, we can know the self as an object. What we cannot do is to make subject and object coincide completely— the subject that is now the object of my reflection is the subject of previous acts, not the subject who is now reflecting.

To come to know oneself as a subject, on the other hand, is to abstain from assaulting oneself as an observer or an analyzer. It is to learn a technique of reflection not patterned on the techniques by which we come to know objects. It is to "take possession of oneself," not as an enemy storming the walls from outside, but as one who already is oneself, but who needs to *become aware* of who one is. Aggressiveness is not needed; peace is needed. One must, perhaps, fight one's way outside the categories and methods used for objects, so as not to think of oneself as an object.

Some succeed in this battle if they simply relax and let the techniques for dealing with objects fall from their hands. Others need to untrain themselves, to decondition themselves, with more attention; for they find that the impulse to objectify themselves is greater than their ability to take themselves as subjects. Some are so habituated to thinking of everything as an object, that they find it baffling to imagine what a "subject" is: they look for another object.

The primary task of philosophy, let us repeat, is to lead its students to knowledge of themselves as subjects. Made into a different kind of man by this knowledge, the philosopher attempts to express this knowledge in words. In the light of his self-knowledge, he tries then to relate objects of the world to other objects and to himself. There is a knowledge of things as they are related to each other; there is a knowledge of things as they are related to the senses, desires, needs, and purposes of men; there is, thirdly, a knowledge of oneself as subject.[2] It is the last that is the source of the other two, although it is more common for philosophers to concentrate upon the other two. We shall wish to concentrate upon the source, which in some way affects everything else—in some way *is* everything else.[3]

For a philosopher does well to concentrate upon intelligent subjectivity, that nest of preconceptions, drives, desires, pre-suppositions, and canons by which he understands whatever he understands. The philosopher need not visualize himself only as a man who steps back from the phenomena he studies, in order to take an objective look; nor as a physicist coolly reading certain instruments; nor as a logician shaping postulates and inventing languages; nor as an analyst of verbal puzzles. The philosopher takes himself as a man; he sees, learns, smells, touches things. He meets other men. He is a person inserted in history, reflecting as he experiences. The philosopher is not a pure, rational ego "inside" a body trying to argue his way out into the external world, or to convince himself that there are other minds, or that other pure egos inhabit the bodies he observes. The philosopher is not a pure, isolated consciousness standing outside of history, *sub specie aeternitatis*; nor, on the other hand, isolated inside a body behind its phenomenal screen. He is a subject, alive and aware in the flux into which he has been born. He is in the world; he becomes himself through commerce with things, and things become real for him through being known by him. He is the crossroad where the world of objects and the world of subjects are one.

The canons of simplicity, parsimony, and elegance, which lead men to prefer one conceptual system to another, for example, are not empirical generalizations about "the structure of the human mind," nor are they elements of "empirical psychology." Yet such canons are operative in the behavior of those who use scientific method, and this fact raises questions about the relation of scientific inquiry to other human behavior. Do men always prefer simplicity and elegance? Do men fall in love by scientific method, or make intelligent decisions in business, politics, or friendship by its canons? Do some men deliberately reject such canons, seek the irrational, and even act against their self-interest? The fact that men in science do behave according to such canons may not, moreover, be an isolated fact. It may, for example, give ground for an inference that these canons are not merely happy, isolated formulations. They may arise, rather, as the mind's proper response to the intelligible and statistical order of the world. The canons of scientific inquiry articulate part of the conscious life of men. They seem to be determined by the subject who articulates them, by his purposes, and by the objects he is trying to know. They are stated impersonally; but they arise out of, are decided upon by, and seriously affect the person who abides by them.

Both the impersonal formulations of science and the business-like, metaphorical language of common sense, however, serve to disguise from us the importance of intelligent subjectivity. We are easily led to think ourselves other than we are, and to be caught in the daily labor of forgetfulness. Ordinary language dulls our sense of discrimination; it has been developed for ordinary purposes: for the pointing out of objects, the exchange of goods, the conduct of political, economic, and familial life. Ordinary language is a language of objects: of him and her and it. Only in personal encounter, in the use of "I" and "you" are there hints in ordinary language that the world in which men live is not only a world of objects, but also of conscious persons. But in the routine of everyday life, men are treated as objects; and even "I" and "you" are often taken in senses not far removed from the sense of "it." Often we treat one another as machines, as officials in certain impersonal roles; it is increasingly rare that we respond to one another as persons. Bus drivers, salesgirls, secretaries, cleaning people, taxi drivers, clients, students, acquaintances: these are all useful objects to us, on whom we spend a minimum of personal consideration.

Only rarely do we meet someone's eyes, or enter into friendship or begin to disclose our hopes, in such a fashion that businesslike conventions are ruptured and two personalities begin to reveal themselves to each other. Even so, we then lack for words. Ordinary language is not made for person-to-person experience. Moreover, since personal consciousness is the starting place of inquiry about God, ordinary language is nearly mute about the origins of belief in God, and even when it does speak its speech tends to make the subject world over into another, vaguer object world. Very few from among ordinary people are interested in the theoretical problems of subjectivity; ordinary language has almost no direct resources for the inquiry after God. Ordinary language is from a religious point of view, furthermore, inherently idolatrous. It makes belief in God into a function of human business, and the religious organization into another social pressure group.

In most contexts of ordinary language, it is possible to accept life on a pragmatic basis, upon utilitarian considerations. One can use the weight of these contexts to argue that the remaining contexts are "mythical." In England and America, such a philosophical orientation has given rise to a large measure of freedom for the individual person in a political system of great practical wisdom.[4] But when the individual person has been granted such freedom since birth, he sometimes wishes to ask, "What shall I do with it?" If the answer is, "Maximize pleasure for yourself and others," he may wish to inquire, "What kinds of pleasure should I introduce myself to, and learn to like?" If the answer is "Experiment and please yourself," he may reply, "Has the past experience of men no guidance to offer me? Life is short; how can I go most quickly to the best that life offers? For my problem is that I do not know, at first, who I am or what best pleases me."

Moreover, a life according to utilitarian rules may seem to make a man into an instrument of society. He may seem to have a role to fulfill, conditioning to be resigned to, an environment to adjust to. Of himself, he may seem more "shaped" than "shaping." His efforts at controlling history are likely to be extroverted: establishing, reforming, or destroying institutions according to his purposes. There seems to be a hollowness at the heart of pragmatic and utilitarian life. Socially, one is forever espousing causes that promise to establish, reform, or destroy institutions; privately, one adapts oneself to one's own conditioning and peer groups. Social idealism and private resignation: bourgeois morality in reverse.

Is there not in some men, at least, a drive for personal moral excellence? And should it not be furthered? Despite what society approves or disapproves, does a man not sometimes wish to be faithful to a vision of his own? I need criteria by which to pass judgment upon such visions, and to determine whether, in each case, it is useful, wise, or noble for me to pursue them. For I am beset with contradictory visions of myself. There appears to be no escape from my need to understand who I am.

2. What Is a Man?

There are four experiences of the human person that seem especially important in the quest for one's own identity. These are the experiences of the activities of awareness, insight, reflective judgment and the drive to understand. When he experiences these activities in his life and reflects on them, a man begins to understand how he is different from objects in the world. He begins to recognize at least one root of both his dignity and his fallibility. He also gains a starting place for thinking about God.

The best guide we have for thinking about what God is like, one plausible tradition has it, is the most accurate notion we have of what man is like; in all this universe, the human phenomenon is the most significant. "That I might know Thee, O God, and myself," Augustine prayed. Knowledge of self and the knowledge of God mount, one after the other, in an ascending, alternating spiral; and in proportion as we discover who we are, we are made ready to discover who God is. "Man is made in the image of God," the old tradition says. In order to know God, where better can man begin than with a more accurate knowledge of himself?

To state fully what he means when he says "God" a man would have to (1) narrate many of his experiences (at prayer, in worship, even in secular action), (2) describe the contexts in which he believes he uses the word "God" well, and, above all, (3) enunciate his understanding of human understanding. For what we mean by "understanding" determines what we mean by "man," and what we mean by "man" guides what we mean by "God." It is to the last of these three tasks, then, that we must now turn, the task of deciding what our identity is. Later, we will wish to assert that the experience on which the language of belief is best grounded is the experience a man has of himself as a subject. Now we must ask, What is the experience of oneself as a subject?

It is, in the first place, like no other experience. Many fail to notice it because their attention is focused on other experiences, or because they look for it as if it were like other experiences. It is the conscious experience of presence to one's self, the radical and fundamental awareness that underlies all our other experiences or ways of knowing. Yet this "self" that is experienced is not intuited directly, nor introspected, nor posited as an hypothesis, nor otherwise known according to the ways by which we know objects. A good account of it is given, together with an analysis of the presuppositions of those who overlook it (or who, like Professor Gilbert Ryle in *The Concept of Mind*,[5] deny it), by J. R. Lucas in his essay "The Soul" in *Faith and Logic*.[6] It is the experience of being oneself and no other; it is the experience of being conscious and alert. This experience can be poignant, even startling, as when one has long been involved in activities that take one's attention elsewhere and then suddenly becomes restfully aware of one's self, apart from all the activity, at ease and uninvolved. But the experience can also be much more prosaic. At any moment, a man may note that he is aware of himself differently from the way in which he is aware of objects "outside" him, or of words or thoughts "inside" him. The experience of awareness is accessible to all; but each must become aware of it for himself: become, as it were, aware of his own awareness.

The basic experience of awareness may be made to emerge in consciousness, for example, if one reflects quietly upon such themes as the following: How do I know that I am I? Do I remember having been younger, slimmer, less sophisticated, less wise than I now am?. . . . When I am asked a difficult question, how do I know that it is the same I who (1) hears the words of the question, (2) understands their point, (3) tries to recollect all the related data, (4) sorts out the relevant data, (5) formulates an answer that the questioner will find intelligible, (6) answers vocally?

The life of consciousness is complex and intense. Its heart seems to be the sense of self-identity, which we may call simple or first awareness. Even if we do not speak about the self, that conscious center of unity is alive and operative in everything we do. It can be made, by such experiences as the above, doubly conscious. We can become conscious of being conscious, aware of being aware. Each of us, it appears, is a subject, a person, a center of consciousness, whether we reflect on our subjectivity or not, whether we are conscious of our consciousness or not.

Moreover, the experience of being aware is a condition of and is prior to all other experience. It is a cognitive experience, but it is not a looking, nor a reasoning, nor a reflecting. It is so simple an awareness that it is difficult to describe in words. In describing it, one is forced to describe some other act, in which indirectly and as by a certain overriding awareness the knower is aware of his own identity even as he performs the other act. Thus one is led to distinguish two forms of awareness.[7] First awareness is simple, indirect, unreflective. It is common to the learned and unlearned, the sophisticated and the unself-conscious. Through it, one is simply "present to oneself." One wants to say, "Me—remembering and imagining and reasoning—through all my experience, *me*."

The challenge "How do you know that you're you?" may exasperate the unlearned. But a sophisticated reply is available: there is no other knowledge prior to self-awareness by which self-awareness can be criticized. For if there were not this latent self-awareness, how could a man be sure that he had heard the sentence he is now criticizing, or that he once learned the reasons on which he now bases his criticism?

Simple awareness is the bedrock of subjectivity, of personality, of self-identity. It is best understood, perhaps, as opposed to unconsciousness: unconscious, we are not present to ourselves.

To be first-aware of sunlight and a breeze streaming through one's hair and a lake glistening out beyond a pier, one need not be aware of being aware: it suffices that one be present and awake, and that the sun be shining, a breeze blowing, and a lake glistening in the foreground of one's vision.

Awareness in the second sense, second awareness, is more recondite, self-conscious, analytic, and usually verbal. We call attention to ourselves as first-aware; we become second-aware that we are first-aware. This second kind of awareness might be called self-consciousness or reflectiveness. It is akin to other forms of knowing: investigative, analytic, ratiocinative; but it is introverted rather than extroverted, and makes even of the self an object. It is because of this second sense of awareness that the first kind is overlooked and its special nature ordinarily unnoticed. Second awareness is indispensable if we are to talk about ourselves as objects in a philosophical system or in any other verbal context at all. But it derives its empirical justification from the prior, simpler, unreflective first awareness that is not investigative, analytic, or ratiocinative like other forms of knowing.

It is above all important to note that first awareness, unlike second awareness, is not a form of looking or observing: we do not intuit, see, or grasp the self as an object. Rather, in being first-aware *or* second-aware of objects—looking at a tree or at a page of print, touching a table, thinking of a problem, making a decision—we have an indirect sense of being awake, alive, and ourselves. This indirect sense is a first awareness of the self, an awareness by which we are conscious, able to deal with objects, and at the same time first-aware of our own identity. First awareness is the arena in which objects meet the subject, and that is why it is prior to second awareness. To become alert to the exercise and implications of first awareness is to enter the depths of subjectivity: of freedom, self-criticism, and adjustment to the claims of objects. Subjectivity is the ground of objectivity. Rationalist philosophers, both idealists and pragmatists, commonly neglect this ground.

First awareness is susceptible of many gradations in accordance with the complexity of man's inner life. We are first-aware of ourselves in various ways: when we are harboring idle thoughts, are aroused to face a practical problem, hit upon a solution, decide to act upon it. From a quiescent state, we can thus call our powers increasingly into operation. At each step, since each includes and depends upon the ones that have gone before, we become "more ourselves," and correspondingly more "self-possessed."

First awareness in its fullness unifies sense, imagination, inquiry, insight, decision, activity, and enjoyment of success or acknowledgment of failure. It does so even when this first awareness is not analytic or reflective; i.e., is not second awareness. We are first-aware of our identity, whatever the activity in which we are engaged. One need not be analytic or reflective in order to live and act as a subject; all of us interiorly are subjects.

It is important to stress the fact that first awareness is cognitive. It is so much so that it is proper to speak of "intelligent" or "rational" subjectivity rather than of "irrational" or "emotive" subjectivity. First awareness is not emotive, even though it is "subjective." There are two senses of "subjective," one meaning "noncognitive" or "emotive"; and that is not the sense in question here. First awareness is subjective because it is not extroverted nor introverted, turned outward upon public objects or inward upon phenomena susceptible of "objective" behavioral analysis; it is concerned with the self, its alertness, and its identity. The self, in other words, is not an object, not even an "inner" one, and cannot entirely and adequately be known as one.

Nevertheless, first awareness is cognitive, inasmuch as it may be experienced by every man, inasmuch as various hypotheses may be advanced to "explain" this experience (or to explain it away), inasmuch as rules of evidence may be advanced for establishing which of those hypotheses satisfy the claims of the experience, and inasmuch as first awareness is required for all these posterior cognitive activities. To deny first awareness, one must employ it. First awareness is required for criticizing oneself in the light of reason. First awareness is thus the cognitive act most proper and intimate to a person, assuring him of his own identity through all the range of his actions; and it is, among cognitive acts, *sui generis*. It is subjective, yet cognitive; private, yet common to every person; accessible to every man for verification in himself, and utterly indispensable in other cognitive acts. The mistake of many treatments of knowing is to interpret subjectivity in terms of the emotions (feelings of awe, alienation, wonder, and the like) instead of in terms of rational first awareness. Primarily and above all, the experience of subjectivity is cognitive; but it is not easily expressed in a language created for our use in living among objects.

It may be wise to repeat here a point made earlier. The self is not an object like the objects of common sense or those of science; it is not a table, a new planet, an inner man inside an outer man. Neither is it adequately known in the direct manner by which we observe objects. It is conscious, alert, alive, but it is not a "thing." Moreover, when philosophers begin to speak about the self, or ego, or transcendental unity of apperception, or *en-soi* or *pour-soi*, they almost without exception are making of the self an object that can enter into their theory of objects. A careful analyst or empiricist looks for this object, and does not find it; he tries to develop a theory that does not need such an hypothesis. He thus remains in the universe of objects. But he is himself a subject, alive, alert, and present to himself. He may not have an explanation for consciousness. But he has the experience. He is more of a mystery to himself than his theory of objects allows him to recognize, and every time he acts he uses the first awareness his theory neglects.

There are some philosophers who become alarmed by considerations of subjectivity; they try to remove them entirely from philosophy. For such philosophers, the objective manner of discussing questions of personal identity involves imagining a given human life as a space-time "worm" stretched out through the years of that life-time, and moving from place to place according to the movements of the person. At a certain moment, from this external point of view, an observer may be able to say that the space-time worm jumps into a swimming pool. Now first awareness is what enables the person who jumps into the pool to say, "*I* jumped into the pool," and to feel the water and the sunlight, to be able to be aware of his own past, and the like. To say, moreover, "A part of my space-time worm has jumped into the pool," is from his point of view not quite accurate. It does not express his sense of his own identity; it does not express his first awareness.

On the other hand, first awareness must be distinguished from other conscious activities; it overrides or undergirds, accompanies or makes possible, such other activities. Add to first awareness empirical attention, and conscious activity is intensified: perception of colors, shapes, or objects occurs. Add intelligent attention, and questions arise. (It is at this point that second awareness occurs.) In this way first awareness is, in a metaphor, the base or the context of other conscious activity. It provides the sense of identity and the unifying consciousness which makes personal remembering, experiencing, understanding, reflecting, and deciding possible. Yet it seems that one cannot become directly conscious of first awareness; one can reach it only indirectly, by reflecting on those other conscious activities of which it is a part.

Moreover, there is something misleading in trying to analyze this basic experience; the analysis is complicated and recondite, whereas the experience itself is most common and ordinary. Anyone who is aware of being himself and no other, of experiencing for himself sights and sounds, of acquiring his own insights, of making his own decisions, understands well enough the reality of first awareness. To experience first awareness is one thing; to advert to it another; to find words for it, and to analyze it, a third.

Metaphysics is based on the reality of first awareness, the

awareness that the human subject has of himself as subject. This experience is the bedrock of human life.[8] It cannot be adequately said, only revealed, only shown, because it is prior to words or problems. The perennial drive to understand this awareness has here its empirical base: subjects are not in all respects like objects. Man stands in two worlds; he desires to understand things *and* himself. It is here that Albert Camus[9] located the absurd: in the cold, arctic fact that he was, unlike a tree or a cat, conscious. The absurd arose for him, then, in the confrontation between the nostalgia of this consciousness for total light and the silence it meets in the universe. "It seemed to me for this sunset hour," John Updike wrote in the last story of his collection *Pigeon Feathers*,[10] "that the world is our bride, given us to love, and the terror and joy of the marriage is that we bring to it a nature not our bride's." When philosophy does not speak of this awareness, literature soon does. The empirical philosophy that overlooks it is not adequate to human experience.

Ordinary people, however, are caught in the predicament of being unable to articulate the most complex of their experiences. They borrow from the object-language of their workaday lives even when they speak of matters closest to them as persons. Their moral language borrows from the language of business and law. Their religious language borrows from the language of familial, regal, and legal relationships. Their language of love borrows from poetry, or more often still from silence and the symbols of kiss and embrace. Their minds glide easily from a metaphor to a reality, without distinguishing which aspects are relevant to which. Thus they are peculiarly unprepared for metaphysics. The halo of ordinary usage that accompanies such words as person, order, God, obligation, and the like enables them to understand something of what the metaphysician undertakes to question. But these ordinary words buckle when the weight of philosophical analysis is placed upon them.

This failure of language does not seem to disrupt the religious belief of many people, because they sense that such belief is rooted in the ultimate independence of the human subject from the world of objects. Religious persons borrow language from the object world because they have no other. But their intention is fixed on their awareness of the subject "world."[11] They have an inarticulate awareness of the surabundance of subjectivity, not to be characterized by a list of predicates from the object language howsoever long. Subjectivity is prior to language. I am a person before I can speak. I may not become second-aware of myself as a person until after I have become first-aware of the world; but in our theories we often recognize second awareness before adverting to first awareness. It may also be true that only through language, only through meeting with another as other, am I awakened to myself, taught to articulate and thereby enabled to differentiate myself from the world. It is through language that I come to understand my relation to the world of things and persons as one conscious person among many. But even in the encounter between two speakers, the subjectivity of each is prior to verbal communication, and whatever understanding is to be achieved through words depends on the stage of comprehension to which the subjects have become alert.

Thus, flowing over, around, and under the world of common sense and science is the "world" of subjectivity, the "world" of persons, the experience each man has of being himself. Common sense and science are the coin of social and technical communication. But they do not suffice to communicate empathy, communion, personality; indicative sentences do not suffice for communication between persons. Thus art, morality, love, action, politics, and religion overflow the language of indicatives, sending along on those poor verbal ducts only so much information as is required to defend against factual misunderstanding. Human beings feel tongue-tied because their tongues suffice for conveying impressions of the object-world but not for the communication of the intelligent subjectivity of persons.

It is characteristic of the positivist to remain intellectually in the object-world and to dismiss the remainder as noncognitive. His interpretation of his experience seems inadequate; he overlooks first awareness, and seems to misjudge the variety of the modes of his intelligence. His own inner life seems to offer empirical data by which to modify his theory.

Who am I? At least this: I am a self, conscious and alert. I have an abiding awareness of my own identity, which I can neglect in the divertissement of daily living. Or I can advert to this awareness often and make it the central, guiding experience of my inner life. I can forget, or I can remember.[12]

It is this awareness, it appears, that allows me to initiate long inquiries, form plans, and establish policies. It is this awareness that lights up the otherwise single events of my conscious life with a steady light. Today I reap the fruits of studies undertaken years ago; tomorrow I hope to attain what I have decided today to attempt. When I gather my attention and let myself become conscious to myself I become partly aware of what sort of being I am. In recollection, reflecting upon my own first awareness, I begin to discover myself.

There are countless activities of my conscious life that I can go on to discover and classify. There are the emotions of joy, grief, hatred, anger, desire. There are moments of apathy, ennui, weariness, disgust. There are loves that are more like hates, and hates that seem strangely like twisted love. There are velleities, wishes, hopes, plans, connivances, aims. There are fidelity and infidelity, whether to self or to others. There are fantasy, imagination, verbal image, logical relationship. There are reasoning (both inductive and deductive), thinking, inventing, checking, comparing. There are resistance to a certain way of life, alarm at certain words or ideas, discomfort in certain situations, surprising reactions against certain kinds of people or lines of argument. There are trained reflexes, skills, habits, biases, certainties, insecurities. There are ambitions and self-deceptions.

There are, finally, many activities and fruits of activities in my conscious life of which I am scarcely second-aware, whose relationships and mutual interaction I have not yet, and perhaps never shall, come to understand.

But of all these there is one activity of my inner life it seems especially fruitful to try to understand: the activity of understanding. For this activity is the key to any understanding of the others. Only in proportion as through understanding them I come to respect these other activities for what they are, is my conscious life without distortion. So as not to be misled by fantasies, not to nourish warped attitudes, not to deceive myself by subtle stratagems, not to indulge in easy biases, I must in some measure come to know myself and order my inner life fruitfully. Self-understanding is the condition of objectivity; by it alone one detects distorting factors within and without. In any human context, it is no doubt impossible to detect every distortion; the single eye, the pure heart, the dispassionate self-judgment are to be fostered and nourished, but these are not given men at birth. Nevertheless, self-criticism becomes more effective only by a more rigorous use of the same source, which has been less effective, just as a bad use of scientific method is corrected only by a better use. The advantage, moreover, of seizing upon understanding as a starting place for self-knowledge is that there is no activity more searching than understanding, and none which is equally self-revising. To a man who is trying to be faithful to understanding, one can hope to point out bias or distortion—even again and again, to the limit of his fidelity—but with a man who will make no effort to understand his own deficiencies or oversights or presuppositions, communication beyond his present range is finally impossible.

But what do we mean by understanding? First awareness is more basic than understanding. But understanding is that activity most closely related to first awareness. Like first awareness, it is not a looking, an intuiting, a thinking. Like first awareness, it is impossible to describe directly. There is a temptation to use as synonyms for it words referring to the activities of the senses, especially those related to sight and touch: seeing, grasping, observing, regarding, perceiving, and so on. But understanding is distinctive precisely because it is unlike these other activities. To understand is not to take a look, to observe, to see, to perceive. On the other hand, since we seem to understand and to speak according to metaphors taken from the object-world, we have no other words to use except those borrowed from the life of the senses. Regularly, philosophers appeal to what we intend by understanding; for they speak of "getting the point," "attaining an insight," "coming to the heart of the matter," "seeing the point," "grasping the relationship," "checking a deduction at each step." Similarly, they speak of "solving a problem," "relating this to that," "comparing," "distinguishing," "uniting all the elements," "detecting a pattern," "classifying," "learning a rule." There is even the "inverse insight" of detecting the fact that there is no pattern, no intelligibility, nothing to understand directly, in a "random" occurrence or a merely statistical regularity.[13] For one triumph of modern understanding is to have found ways of dealing with matters classical philosophers (and scientists) would have treated as surds—as irrational, as formless, as patternless. To understand, then, is not only to be able to understand as classical philosophers and scientists understood understanding; it is also to be able to see the point of statistical methods, surds,[14] and such matters as "shaggy dog" stories and motiveless, "meaningless" crimes.

There are two moments in the activity of understanding that it seems important to distinguish. The first is the moment of "appearing to get the point," which we have roughly described in the preceding paragraph, and to which we shall return. The second is the moment of reflective evaluation or verification (*"Have* I got the point, and is it correct?"). For simplicity's sake, we may call the first moment that of insight and the second that of reflection; or the first moment that of making a claim and the second that of justifying the claim. These names are only shorthand; neither moment is exclusively of one character, nor is either completely different from the other. In both moments, the point sought by inquiry must emerge in consciousness; in both moments, the conditions set by the demands of inquiry must be met. But the second moment is the completion of the first, and more complex than the first.

Neither moment of understanding is to be understood apart from inquiry. To understand is to possess the answer to a question; it is to have satisfied, however momentarily, an appetite to see the point and to be sure that one has seen it. Every man sometimes understands, and no one boasts of never having understood anything. Every man has sometimes had a question. If anyone doubts that he has, the very doubt raises the question. A question, moreover, is sometimes an explicit "Why?" or "What?" but often, too, it is merely an inarticulate, intelligent interest. Not all men are equally inquisitive; not all allow this particular appetite its full development in their personalities. It appears, further, that many flee from understanding when other appetites threaten to be contradicted by it: comfort, convenience, habit, interest of another kind, security, commitment, complacency. On the other hand, many admire a man who understands what he is doing, who is regularly faithful to understanding, who follows—whether in inquiry or in action—whither his understanding leads him. One is tempted to say that *he* is the real man. One is tempted to revise the classical tag from "man is a rational animal" to "man is an animal who understands."[15] If praise and blame are a clue, we may see in understanding (and in fidelity to it) the basic human activity. "Stupid" is the most undercutting insult of all, disqualifying a man from most of the things we expect of him.

First awareness, moreover, is the base from which understanding appears to start; it is because we are conscious as subjects that we are able to raise questions. The appetite characterized by intelligent attention, or by the raising of explicit questions, seems to be the dynamism that propels our intellectual and our moral life; according as we nourish that appetite, we grow in intellectual and in moral penetration. Our acts of understanding, therefore, have a base in first awareness, and a dynamic thrust in the drive of inquiry; they are not static, and they are not discontinuous. Finally, as an empirical fact, understanding does occur. No reader would have gotten so far along in this book had not many acts of understanding occurred during his reading; and were there not on his part a curiosity to discover the resolution of remaining questions. Without the base in first awareness, no questions would be possible. Without the drive to understand, no further questions would attract one's interest, and no further acts of understanding would or could occur.

Through the first moment of understanding (which we are calling "insight") a man finds emerging in his consciousness the response to an initial stimulus to his intelligence: he sees the solution to his problem, discovers a way of relating the puzzling clues, hits on the correct word for his crossword puzzle, gets the point of a joke, after hours of work comes upon the premise that allows him to construct the requisite deduction in a problem of logic, at last catches a professor's meaning after having heard him repeat the point through a semester, gains insight into the puzzling character of an acquaintance,[16] comes to see that his own behavior has been locked in certain heretofore unconscious patterns, discerns a business trend from a welter of statistics, shrewdly estimates from past experiences the difficulties he will have with a certain client, grasps the political compromise that will keep competing interests in equilibrium, chooses for communication the words best calculated to prompt the desired insights to emerge in the consciousness of others, wordlessly comes to know that the color he is now adding to his canvas, rather than the color he has just tried, best contributes to the visual image he desires. Insight is required for many tasks, plays many roles. It is often wordless and nonconceptual. Of itself, in fact, it is prior to concepts and words; through conditioning, parrots and schoolboys can be led to use words correctly without it. But in the daily work of human intelligence, insight is central.

But if insight is central, it is not final. It offers the answer to one question, but there is always the further question to be faced: "Is that so?" Not every bright idea is a sound idea, and so understanding as insight is not yet understanding as knowledge. When we have an insight, we do not yet know; intuition is no sure test of truth. In order to complete the second moment of understanding, and put to rest the question that demands the justification for our claim to understand, we must evaluate the evidence we possess.

It seems, at first, that every insight takes place within a finite context. We do not normally raise every possible question in order to decide whether the answer to our present question is correct. Life is short, and after a certain point enough inquiry is enough for the purposes at hand. In practice, then, we set a finite number of conditions which the evidence must meet. For a crossword puzzle, for example, the evidence is usually supplied by the demands of the "down" and the "across" columns, by a dictionary or a friend in emergencies, and in really hard cases by the answer supplied by the creator of the puzzle. But if the answer is not supplied, and if a dictionary or friend is not available, then we must rely on the conditions set by the double columns and on our own verbal acuity. Nevertheless, in either case, the surprising fact is that our finite number of conditions shades off into the infinite. Conceivably, one could raise questions about the correctness of a certain usage that would go far beyond the purposes of the given puzzle, and one could in dissatisfaction leave the spaces blank. But when we are in fact satisfied with the completed puzzle, we may say that our evidence is virtually unlimited; though we have in fact cut the problem down to our size. The demands of "down" and "across," our own verbal skill, the dictionary, the help of others, the general usage that supports the authority of the dictionary, and the puzzle-builder's answer, all concur. At no place does there seem to be a loophole. An infinity of questions could be raised, but in the limited context to which we appeal, no raised and unanswered questions dislodge the letters we pencil into the blocks.

The process of justifying our claim to understand seems to involve, then, a limited universe of inquiry. We raise and answer those obvious and even those less proximate questions that would unsettle our claim; we seek to close off a virtually unlimited set of challenges. It is true that for most purposes, enough is soon enough; we rarely demand, even in professional philosophy, that every conceivable question, from every conceivable viewpoint, be met. On the other hand, however, there is ever the sneaky suspicion that unless every possible condition has been met, we do not truly know that our understanding is correct. For our claim to know seems to involve us in an appeal to the completely unconditioned: "I know that . . ." is not ordinarily tentative. And our completed set of finite conditions seems to imitate the completion of unlimited conditions, or the truly unconditioned; it is a "virtually unconditioned."[17]

In fact, then, our appeal is only to the virtually unconditioned— unconditioned from a certain point of view, after a certain amount of investigation, for certain purposes. But a man who says "I know" and is too often found to have been wrong, and therefore *not* to have known, is soon a man of diminished intellectual credit, since for tentative attainments we ordinarily except tentative claims. It is true that we often allow the context of the claim to qualify its stringency; we recognize that the "I know" is virtually unconditioned, and so accept the gap between the virtually and the simply unconditioned. But, in our stricter moments, we hew the virtually unconditioned as close to the simply unconditioned as possible. For it is the unconditioned that alone *constitutes* the putting to rest of all possible questions, and entitles us to say with strict right, "I know." An indication of this is that the skeptic generally begins by accepting "I know" in its strictest sense, and then shows that men can not so use it, whereas a healthy and critical philosophy seems to begin with the virtually unconditioned that men in fact claim to have fulfilled. It then tries to go on to show that the virtually unconditioned derives its strength from the simply unconditioned, to which it implicitly makes appeal, and toward which it is steadily driven by the relentless drive of inquiry.

In any case, the second moment of understanding is concerned with passing judgment upon the adequacy of the evidence that purports to uphold the claim of the moment of insight; it is concerned with the conditions that must be met if that claim is to be accepted. One set of these conditions involves the knower. What conditions does he set for the evidence, and why? What are his criteria of relevance and evidence? Moreover, the knower will wish to assure himself that he is in a position to know that he has acquired the requisite skills; that his present frame of consciousness is adequate to the task; that the physical and other conditions are "normal"; that he does not usually make mistakes in such matters; that no odd factor seems to be present; and the like.[18] When a man claims to know, he is also making a claim about his own capacities and situation as a knower. Insight into oneself is requisite for correct knowing.

Thus the second moment of understanding presents us with another aspect of intelligent subjectivity. Nothing known objectively except through a knower; and a knower knows objectively only by acquiring the requisite skills, discipline, and qualities of heart and mind. Among such qualities are honesty, preference for accurate judgment over personal interest, not too much haste, avoidance of presumption, and so on. The methodological relativist seems to be correct in pointing out that the foundations of all human knowing lie in the resources of intelligent subjectivity; and that as each man is, so he will judge. There is no direct path to objectivity, through immediate contact with "naked, disguised" impressions, or with spiritual essences, or in any other way. Objectivity is the much-prized achievement of intelligent subjectivity. There is no way to objectivity other than through intelligent subjectivity. It is the knower who decides what he accepts knowing to be, and disposes himself to know.

But if the second moment of understanding is clearly subjective before it is objective, in fact it is often both, since we do accept some judgments as objective. However, the first moment of understanding is quite clearly subjective. The act of insight is highly personal; it is directly dependent on the development and preparation of the subject. A man in an unfamiliar environment will miss the point of local stories; a selfish man will not detect his own prejudices; a novice will not understand problems the expert dispatches easily; the dull attain insight only rarely, the bright frequently. The act of insight, and indeed the capacity for insight, lies at the heart of personality.

For the sake of later discussion this point ought to be emphasized. The act of insight is central in scientific method in the perception of objects, and in ostension or "reasonable induction." But it is also central in the psychological development of the person. Born egocentric, as unself-critical and egocentric as other animals, only gradually does the human being begin to liberate himself by the practice of intelligence from the immediacy of biological drives and needs. Only gradually does he come to explain his own unconscious motivation and complex rationalizations. Only slowly does he earn his way through adolescence and apprenticeship to skill in some human labor, art, or field of scholarship; to good judgment; to reasonable altruism. Not every insight into his own character, however, is accurate; nor does every inquiry in the quest for self-discovery issue in insight. But it is certain that insight, if it is not everything, is central in the Socratic imperative *Know thyself*. As insight is central in science, so it is central in ethics. It is central in every specifically human activity. It is common to all peoples, in all times, however various its modes and the conceptual systems in which it finds expression. Insight, dynamically related to critical reflection and verification, offers one of the useful focal points for a philosophy of intelligent subjectivity.

A philosophy based on concepts and logical system is inherently rationalistic. A philosophy based on intuitions, feelings, will, or pragmatic purposes is inherently irrationalistic. But a philosophy based on the two moments of understanding—the *moment of insight* verified by the *moment of reflection*—seems to coup the advantages of all man's abilities: first awareness, senses, imagination, emotions, habits of mind and heart, creative and critical intelligence, and will. For it aims at and depends upon self-knowledge, tries to respect each of man's abilities and liabilities for what it is, and is self-revising. As soon as a man who is trying to be faithful to understanding discovers an error in his methods or his estimates, it is consistent with his intention and his method to correct that error.

In this sense, there is in such a philosophy a counterclaim against uncritical relativism. One cannot say: "Anything goes." Only that can be approved which meets the conditions laid down by one's own understanding; and if those conditions are found, through experience or argument, to have been laid down unsuitably or even incorrectly, fidelity to understanding requires their revision. Final appeal in such argument cannot be to any abstract criteria or any code of propositions; merely to assert that other criteria or another code are correct is to beg the question. The final positions of wisdom are won only through dialectic, not by deduction. Final appeal can only be made to fidelity to the demands of understanding. Where that fidelity is present, reasonable discourse is possible; where it is absent, appeal to intelligence is irrelevant.

A certain kind of relativism inheres, therefore, in the human situation. But it is not a relativism that ends in solipsism; it is the relativism of intelligent subjects in a community of reasonable discourse. Moreover, those who are faithful to understanding share a community of life, however diverse their actual conceptions, points of view, and criteria of the real. They are one in intention: united in the program of fidelity each to his own understanding, an understanding that is self-critical and self-revising. It is this program that makes dialogue possible.[19]

Our conscious life, then, not only has a base in first awareness; it is also active and searching. It is driven to ask questions and to search out the realities of our experience. This attention and these questions come to tentative rest, if at all, in the insights that they seek, in the intelligible (or the recognition of the lack of it) that they discover. But questions seeking insight are only the first wave of conscious inquiry; insights are not guarantors of truth. After the sought-after solution emerges in our consciousness—after the desired insight is attained—our drive to understand is not complete until it has confirmed the fulfillment of the conditions on which the claim "I understand" is based. Only then can we make the stronger claim, "I know."

Insight is the mediating moment between each of those three acts by which each person relates himself realistically to the world of things and other persons. First comes intelligent attention, or an explicit question put to the data to be understood. Next, sooner or later, comes the mediating insight. Thirdly comes the reflective and completing judgment. Until insight occurs, the data are dumb and shapeless. But insights do not constitute knowing; insight apart from reflective justification does not bring to rest the drive to understand.

Who am I? At least this: I am a subject, aware and alert; I sometimes understand; and I sometimes am able to support with reasons my claim to understand, thus fulfilling the conditions on which such a claim is acceptable, both by myself and others, "objectively." I am an intelligent subject, then, capable of objectivity.

3. *The Drive to Understand*

The third factor of extraordinary importance in our cognitional experience is the drive to understand, manifested in intelligent attention, in the dynamism of inquiry, and in the restless urge to explore new horizons. A man does not appear to be curious as a cat is curious, for the satisfaction of immediate interests. A man sometimes wishes to understand exactly how things are in themselves and apart from his immediate biases; how they tick and what makes them tick. He is sometimes interested in understanding how things are related to his sense-perception, interests, viewpoints, needs, both concretely and in the future or in general. At other times he is interested in how things are related to one another, apart from their relation to him: not in whether it appears to him that the sun goes around the earth, but in the sun's motion relative to the motion of the earth without reference to his point of observation.[20] Through his drive to understand, a man is capable of discounting some of his limitations and interests for the sake of explanatory understanding. The scientific spirit, for example, is striking evidence of the objectivity pursued by the drive to understand, at the expense of other human interests.[21]

What exactly is this drive to understand? It appears to be present in the experience of most men. Any man who wishes to understand his drive to understand has in his own experience the data to be understood. But there are four aspects of those data to which it seems especially useful to draw attention.

In the first place, the drive to understand appears to be, of itself, unstructured. It is not predetermined in such a way that in any one case it must operate in this manner rather than in that. For if one method of inquiry fails, there seems to be nothing to prevent us from searching out and using another method. If one line of investigation does not succeed, we may hope to discover a more fruitful line. So long as there is something to be understood, we seem to be able to revise our preconceptions and our methods until we manage to attain the understanding we seek, or to discover the reason why we cannot attain it. And if we do not reach either of these points, we remain restless and inquisitive.

Thus, behind every concrete line of inquiry there are certain preconceptions. And behind each of these preconceptions, there are other lines of inquiry by which they are supported. Since each of these preconceptions is questionable, we may say that the drive to understand is preconceptual; it does not proceed a priori, but is flexible and open to the demands of each particular inquiry. It is the radical, unstructured *why* at the heart of our conscious life. Preconceptions and lines of inquiry are its tools for specific purposes. In order to understand something, we must begin with some conceptions and some lines of inquiry. But each of these conceptions and each of these lines of inquiry is subject to revision should we change our purposes and/or our direction. The drive to understand is like a source of light rather than like a basic cluster of undeniable, self-evident premises or "pinned-down" statements; premises and statements are its instruments, not its substance.

Secondly, if the drive to understand is unstructured it is also unlimited in its scope. Its goal is to understand, without limit, everything that is to be understood, and even to understand about those things which are unintelligible why they are so. Whatever data men encounter, they may question. When they try to understand what exactly it is that they encounter, and try to relate it to themselves or to other things, they are trying to come to grips with everything in their experience. And there appears to be no point at which one can say, No further. For to question whether one can go beyond a given point is already to have set sights beyond it. The opposite pole of the drive to understand is, then, everything that is to be understood. And that would appear to be everything that is. For there does not seem to be anything that man will or can encounter that he will not wish to question. The horizon of the drive to understand appears to be all of reality, however we might choose to define reality. The horizon of an individual man, of course, is modest and limited; but insofar as he is faithful to his drive to understand he breaks through the limits of his early conditioning, his parochial viewpoint, his personal experiences, his peculiar limitations in space and time, to an ever more cosmopolitan, objective, sympathetic, encompassing horizon. The ideal limit of this development is that he should understand, without limit, all that is to be understood. His drive to understand, however limited in the concrete, is even in its present exercise an intimation of that terminal ideal that is beyond his reach.

In the third place, the drive to understand is objective in intention. It is "objective" not, of course, in the sense that it "makes an object of" but in the sense that its goal is the real rather than the imagined. It is not of itself confined to the biases of the personal subject nor to the conventional wisdom of his peers. Of itself, the drive to understand is relentlessly critical both of the self and of the common sense of its historical community. For in some measure men do succeed in making objective judgments, and in successfully challenging the conventional wisdom, if the light of a more compelling understanding of the data of human experience so directs them. Were the drive to understand not objective in intention, progress in science and morals would have little hope of success. There would be no desire for reasonable discourse, but this man would be content to appeal to his personal inclinations and that man would excuse himself on the grounds that everyone in his group did the same as he. Yet we do not always countenance such appeals, not even when we make them in our own behalf. For the drive to understand summons us to a more stringent bar, before which we are obliged to set forth what we understand to be the case, and the reasons for our so understanding; and further questions are raised both about our understanding and our reasons for it. The implication is that had we not fled from the drive to understand, we would have anticipated these further questions earlier.

It is always open to us to rationalize our flights from understanding. But what is not open to us is to rationalize, and then to declare the further questions of the drive to understand irrelevant. For the appeal to rationalization invites an appeal to further inquiry, since to be reasonable is not to hide from questions but just the opposite: to be subject to the drive to understand. A man can live and act without reasons. But he cannot attempt to justify his living or his acting without inviting further scrutiny from his own accusing drive to understand, abetted by the less circumscribed objectivity of others.

It would not be too much to say that the drive to understand makes possible whatever objectivity men attain in science, in ethics, in politics, in love, or elsewhere in daily life. And the reason that it does so is that it does not seem to be, of itself, corruptible by the biases, interests, and needs of the intelligent subject. The subject, of course, will have a thousand stratagems for deceiving himself and others even in the name of objectivity; there are not, as Pascal says, four honest men in a century. Yet such stratagems, insofar as they can be detected by the subject, must be detected by this inner objective drive; without the drive to understand, they would be neither stratagems nor deceptions but the acceptable standard of human inquiry. Unless there is honesty, there are no deceits.

Political life, of course, for the very reason Pascal gives, cannot be based on the hope that men will each discover their own hypocrisies. For all men, the clash of personal interests and the check-and-balance of wise politicial institutions are required if they are to attain an approximation of objectivity. Still, the drive to understand constitutes by its intention of objectivity both the base and the dynamic of scientific and ethical development and, in a different context and with different purposes in view, the base and dynamic of realistic political judgment. The clear-eyed pragmatist must often appeal to it against his own passions, immediate interests, and prejudices.

Finally, the drive to understand, of itself, supplies the unifying intention of our cognitional life. Of the moments of observation, questioning, hypothesis, and verification, it constitutes a unified inquiry. Of first awareness, intelligent attention, insight, and critical reflection it constitutes one act of knowing. Of otherwise unconnected events, responses, and initiatives, it constitutes a policy. Of otherwise unrelated hopes, desires, aims, and needs, it constitutes a plan of action. Of otherwise separate insights and theories, it constitutes a field of inquiry or a systematic survey. Moreover, it is by our line of inquiry or our policy of action that our attention is ordinarily directed in certain ways rather than in others. The concrete direction in which our drive to understand is currently moving thus affects what we notice and what we overlook.

Since the drive to understand seeks ultimately all that can be understood, the intention of that drive, taken in itself, exceeds the limited goals of limited inquiries. Inasmuch as we proceed toward that ultimate horizon by taking concrete steps in coming to grips with the concrete horizons presently before us, each act of understanding brings with it a certain joy in its appropriation, a certain rest and complacency. But inasmuch as the intention of our drive to understand exceeds such concrete contexts, our joy, rest, and complacency yield again to the rhythm of anxiety, restlessness, and concern inviting us to advance to the further horizon that challenges us.[22]

In his penetrating study *Thought and Action*,[23] Stuart Hampshire offers an analysis of intentionality as it applies to human action, and he centers his analysis on the idea of "trying to do." When a man acts consciously, we expect him to be able to answer the question, "What are you doing?" He may not be able to articulate his answer quickly, nor need he have thought verbally and explicitly about it. But his activity can scarcely be described as conscious if our question is not a proper one. Implied in our notion of action, then, is the idea of intention: a thread of intelligence, perhaps inarticulate, linking together the elements of what we are trying to do. Extending Hampshire's argument, we would wish to suggest that intentionality is also present in our understanding and in our knowing, as well as in our doing.[24]

G. E. M. Anscombe has likewise written a dense but helpful study called *Intention*.[25] And Bernard Lonergan analyzes the drive to understand in some detail under the rubric, "the pure, detached, disinterested, unrestricted desire to know."[26] We may take it, then, that the fact of this drive to understand is sufficiently recognized, and that its analysis is well under way. The goal of the drive to understand is to understand all that can be understood. This intention drives us step by step along the discursive path of human understanding, and lights our way both by policy and by singular decision through the concrete complexities of what we try to do in the world.

Who am I? At least this: an intelligent subject who sometimes understands and who sometimes knows; and a subject whose ultimate horizon is all that is to be understood; whose personal development follows upon fidelity to the drive to understand both in realistic and objective doing, and in realistic and objective knowing; and whose intellectual and moral life advances from horizon to horizon in a rhythm of rest and action.

4 ❖

WHAT DO I MEAN

BY "GOD"?

1. In Prayer

It is plain that most of those who do not believe in God think of him as a stranger, a social fiction, the projection of obscure emotions, or even as a mythical "Big Daddy."[1] When they speak of God, they speak of something to which they feel no personal bond. It is different with those who believe in God. In the conversation of nonbelievers, God is an "it"; among those believers who truly know him (not all who have belief on their lips have belief in their intelligence and heart), God is a "you." One speaks differently of a person, than one does of a thing. Further, one speaks differently *to* a person than merely of him.

It is in prayer that one comes to know God best. To those who do not believe, of course, prayer is an absurdity. But it is not so clear whether prayer is an absurdity because one does not believe in God, or whether one does not believe in God because one does not pray. Belief and prayer are inextricable. To come to recognize God is to become aware of standing in a conscious presence; it is to stand in silent, wordless communication; and this is prayer. To come to believe is to begin to pray. Not to believe is to stand outside a conversation.

Both believer and nonbeliever live in a world of silence; neither one hears "voices," neither one sees God. Naked belief and critical unbelief are materially alike; in both, the human person stands in a cold, arid silence, unable to detect God with senses or imagination or feelings. Both may suffer the anguish of isolation and cosmic abandonment; contrariwise, both may also indulge in the daily forgetfulness which banishes loneliness. Many believers in some moods experience the angst of Continental intellectuals, and in other moods experience the pragmatic contentment of some American intellectuals. Prayer is not a question of moods.

One prays by intelligence. The experiences of first and second awareness, of insight, of reflective judgment and decision, of the unlimited drive to understand, lead one to pray, and guide one's prayer. By such experiences, and these alone, we recognize that we are persons and not merely objects, that experience is at least partly intelligible, that our unlimited drive to understand can discredit idols and fantasies. In such experiences, the whole dynamic structure of philosophical religious belief is anticipated. Driven by such experiences, one prays.

It is quite possible, of course, to recognize such experiences and not to pray, nor to believe in God. At moments, in the silence, even the believer may be inclined to think that the absurdity of the human situation lies precisely in the fact that man is an intelligent subject, driven by a relentless drive to understand, yet is by some inexplicable happenstance caught in the web of events, bandied back and forth for a while, and then extinguished. Perhaps so. Certainly so, some would say; grow up, and face it.

It is not yet the time to decide between belief and unbelief. First, it is important to try to make clear to ourselves what we mean when we say "God."

I think those philosophers are correct who stand in the tradition of St. Augustine and St. Bonaventure—Dom Illtyd Trethowan has collected testimonies from many of them[2]—who seek God within and through the human spirit. The question, then, is what I take the human spirit to be. In a word, spirit is inquiry, and its first manifestation is the question.[3] Correspondingly, I take God to be the source of both the unrest and the rest of my spirit: the prompter of the drive to understand, and its fulfillment. The critical drive that leads me to give attention, to seek intelligibility, and to criticize insights acquired, is of God; and nothing will give it rest but he alone. He is before the beginning of every question, and he remains after every answer. Our words do not suffice to describe him, nor can our concepts circumscribe him. Nevertheless, we inquire; and the relentless drive that is before every inquiry, and that recognizes the limits of every answer, is our anticipation of his nature.

Moreover, the difficulties of human language in speaking about God are not surprising. Not all the "linguistic therapy" in the world will make speech about God as plain and facile as we should like. Language that is formed for pragmatic purposes, or for the requirements of industry, the professions, and the home, is wrenched out of familiar channels when it is used of God. Language that is sharpened for philosophical purposes, pulled fine and thin for exact conceptual purposes, is more fitted for the needs of the system of which it is a part than for speaking of him who is reached not by any system, but by the anticipations of that dynamic drive that builds, revises, discards, and moves beyond every system. Moreover, even the language that seeks to make explicit and conscious what occurs implicitly in the polymorphic consciousness of those who believe seems to many too naked, too cold, too arctic for their hearts and imaginations. Some believers, for example, insist that they do not conceive of God anthropomorphically, and that sense, emotions, imagination, and conceptual reason cannot reach him; they then protest that a language constructed to avoid these pitfalls creates an air too thin for them to breathe. Their courage fails, and thus they contribute to the deep-seated fear of the heights so characteristic of our century. As the linguistic air becomes rarefied, many men turn back toward the plains of nonbelief.

Those, however, who fear the illusions of evasion more than

the risks of articulation have no choice but to press on. If a language adequate for authentic philosophical belief is to be constructed, then those concerned must be ready to face difficulties and to explore unaccustomed places. We have seen that the instrumentalist language of the pragmatist,[4] as well as the ordinary metaphorical language decried by the author of *Honest to God*,[5] encounter fatal difficulties if employed in the quest for personal identity and the quest for God. For some three centuries, classical philosophy has attempted to make up these deficiencies by employing the language of ontology. Many religious people find this language offensive and misleading.

Reinhold Niebuhr, for example, strenuously resists the employment of the language of ontology, although his friend and former colleague Paul Tillich criticizes him for that resistance. In a volume dedicated to studies about Niebuhr, Tillich complains that Niebuhr rejects the description of man as a rational animal and, in this rejection, "presupposes a concept of reason which has been peculiar to us since the middle of the nineteenth century but which is far removed from the classical concept of reason as it appears, for example, in Stoicism."[6] Tillich continues: "We may call the latter the logos-type of reason: reason seen as an element within the divine life, the principle of his self-manifestation to himself and to everything separated from him. Reason in this sense is the universal power of form and meaning. It is present in the structures of reality and in the structures of the mind which correspond with one another, and which make knowledge . . . possible."[7] It will be fruitful to participate further in this debate.

Tillich accuses Niebuhr of failing to distinguish this "high" concept of reason from "the calculating type of reason," whose origin Tillich traces to Aristotle and which is as old "as man's ability to make a tool." In the eighteenth century, Tillich notes, the classical, or high, concept of reason was still alive. "This 'critical reason' of the 'enlightened' philosophers was a derivative of reason as logos. Slowly, however, this foundation disappeared. Reason was reduced to the cognitive function. It became technical reason: scientific, calculating, arguing. Niebuhr is right when he denies the ability of reason, in this sense, to attain knowledge of God."[8] But, Tillich suggests, "reason is more than arguing reason."[9]

Tillich believes that Niebuhr cannot avoid the question of ontology by seeking refuge in the concept of the self. "In the moment in which one forms concepts like *self* and *dynamics* and *history*, one has left the innocence of the mythological question and must answer the question of God's being in contrast to any finite being."[10] He sees the root of Niebuhr's difficulties in a misreading of philosophic history: "Being, according to his understanding, is necessarily static because it abstracts from everything finite and changing. This may be the case in some types of ontological thought. But it is not true of the predominant trend in ontology. . . . If being is understood as the power of being, the contrast between static and dynamic disappears . . . ."[11] Tillich generalizes his indictment: ". . . in every theological assertion an ontological assertion is included . . . it is one of the tasks of theology to elaborate explicitly its implied ontology . . . ."[12]

Dr. Niebuhr's response to Tillich is direct: "Tillich thinks my difficulty is that I have confused the modern idea of reason ('calculating reason') with the classical type of reason ('*logos* type'). This is a serious misunderstanding on Tillich's part. It is with the classical rationalism that I am chiefly concerned. I do not depreciate it. I know that God must be reason or have reason of the type Aristotle ascribes to the divine. The human self also has this *logos* type of reason as part of its unique creative power. But the self has a freedom which cannot be equated with this reason; and God has freedom beyond the rational structure."[13] He adds: "The idea of creation points to a mystery beyond any system of rational intelligibility."[14] Moreover, ontology "has its limitations in describing any being or being *per se* which contains mysteries and meanings which are not within the limits of reason. Among these are both the human self in its mystery of freedom within and beyond the structure of the mind, and the divine mystery . . . ."[15] Niebuhr admits that the classical type of reason is necessary and useful in order to understand structure and form. "My point is simply that when we deal with aspects of reality which exhibit a freedom above and beyond structures, we must resort to the Hellenic dramatic and historical way of apprehending reality."[16] The crucial sentence follows later: "For nothing in history follows 'in a necessary manner,' that is, either logically or in terms of efficient cause, which could be proved 'necessary' by scientific verification."[17]

It is plain that Professor Niebuhr understands the classical sense of reason in terms of two notions: structure and necessity. For him, the realm of being which is known by reason in the classical sense is ruled by necessities and structures. In the name of ongoing, undetermined history, in the name of the self and of God, he rejects the relevance of classical reason to the core of religious experience.

Professor Tillich, on the other hand, appears to read the classical tradition through the eyes of the Stoics and of the German Enlightenment of the eighteenth century. His preferred sense of reason is "the universal power of form and meaning."[18] He sees reason as the principle of God's "self-manifestation to himself and to everything separated from him."[19] This view of reason is not that, for example, of Aquinas,[20] and it appears not to apply to the ontological language of the tradition that intervenes between the Stoics and the Enlightenment. This difference in ontological languages, particularly concerning the meaning of "necessary" in Aristotle and in Aquinas, presents a puzzle to contemporary analysis.[21] It would take us too far afield to show how our own findings differ from those of both Professor Tillich and Professor Niebuhr. With the former, we can agree that every theology implies an ontology, but we would add that every ontology implies a cognitional theory. With the latter, we can agree that ontology of the classical type is at least misleading because of the connotations of form, structure, and necessity which cling to it.

Moreover, the "freedom" to which Professor Niebuhr appeals seems intimately related to what we are calling the drive to understand, in its critique of structures, and in its restlessness with finite answers. The "universal power" to which Professor Tillich appeals may well be the same drive, but seen from the objective side, from the side of content: the-power-of-making-intelligible, whose work intelligence detects. Tillich's "power of being" appears likewise to be a projection of the drive to understand, a content that transcends "being" as the drive to understand transcends the concepts to which its finite inquiries give rise.[22]

The difficulty with ontology, however, is that it seems to be speaking about objects which are out there to be seen, seen *spiritually*, seen *within* things. And minds of an empirical temper find nothing there to be seen. On the other hand, every statement in ontology can be translated into a statement in cognitional theory.[23] In this way, the language of ontology can be tested. For its source can lie nowhere else than in our powers of cognition. The language of ontology, then, appears to be of no special use in an investigation that undertakes the more radical inquiry into cognitional experience.

We are left in the end with our own hours of prayer, our own sometimes lonely confrontations with the darkness in which God may or may not lie hidden. Conversations with friends, the reading of books, the often inarticulate passing along of a tradition, have often been sturdy guides; no man searches wholly alone. But in the end each man *is* alone in the silence. In that silence, words, images, concepts, representations of all sorts fall away. What, then, are the powers of intelligence? In that dark night, what can intelligence do?

The arguments of nonbelievers do not easily impress one who has grown accustomed to long hours of aridity, emptiness, and voicelessness in prayer. He knows that God is hidden. He adheres to God with a will purified of childhood conditioning, friendly images or images of any kind, emotional comfort, or any creaturely prop. Whatever his sensibilities might propose to him cannot be God. Seeking God, he quite literally expects to detect nothing.[24] Not only does he call no object before his mind, he even knows that whatever object might appear there is not God. On the other hand, he believes that God is conscious, understands, and communicates his presence, though with a communication scarcely to be distinguished from no communication at all. There is no voice, not necessarily any consolation in the heart, perhaps only an unbroken darkness and aridity. But when the believer at prayer rests in this aridity and emptiness, setting his will nakedly toward the God he cannot see, his intelligence is at peace. The fact of this peace is indisputable. It survives the restlessness of the critical, conceptual intelligence, which wishes to see before it believes. For the intelligence so at rest is able to detect the limits of conceptual intelligence, and is able to safeguard itself against the idols of the imagination and the sensibilities,[25] and against the fanaticisms of partial causes. It is, and knows itself to be, safely at rest. "*E la sua volontate è nostra pace:* In His will, our peace." (*Par.* iii 85). One can rest, without seeing, in the hidden God and not fear illusion. In prayer it is so, experimentally.

But how can one explain this to the nonbeliever, so as to uncover the nerve of the decision between belief and unbelief in that great darkness? And how is one to explain it to oneself?

2. Rules for a Language about God

There are two questions to be distinguished in the inquiry about God. The first is the question concerning what language about God means. The second is the question of deciding whether there are sufficient reasons to affirm that belief in God is a *true* belief; whether, that is, one knows that there is a God. At present, we are concerned only with the first of these two questions. And in the light of our reflections upon our own identity and upon prayer, we are prepared to make several proposals about the interpretation of a language of philosophic belief.

The rules that seem to offer useful and accurate guides for human language about God are derived from our cognitional experience: from first awareness, insight, reflection, and the drive to understand. Our first assertion is that *the experience on which religious language is best grounded is the experience a man has of himself as a subject.* Our second assertion is that *of all the experiences of intelligent subjectivity, the one most suitable as a guide to our thinking about God seems to be that of intelligent consciousness, including insight and critical reflection.* At the moment, we forego all discussion of how to conceive of God's will or his activity. Our account must be piecemeal, and hence somewhat unsatisfactory: as unsatisfactory as when a friend submits us to too much analysis, too little direct attention. But analysis is for the sake of a more intelligent relationship, and is useful if it leads to more realistic understanding.

The experience of awareness is so different from any other experience a man shares, seems so alien to the world of objects, that he is forced to explain it to himself. The characteristic of this experience is that it is not extroverted, not totally involved in the stimuli of the object world, nor always driven by sensitive needs to accomplish pragmatic tasks. It is present when men withdraw, relax, are at peace, seem to "live apart" from the rush and drives of the object world; for this reason, when heightened by restful attention, it is sometimes thought of as contemplative. On the other hand, this first awareness is intensified by a dynamic drive; a hunger to understand. Men reflect on the world around them, and on themselves. Their awareness is self-critical; it sometimes recognizes its own rationalizations and the flight by which it tries to blind itself to its egocentric tendencies. The ordinary person is usually inarticulate about such matters, and most often so preoccupied with the object world as to neglect them. But sometimes they are borne in upon him: sitting silent under a lamp on a dark winter evening; alone under the stars; like Tolstoi's Andrey fallen on a battlefield beneath the great sky. At such moments, he is aware of "living in two worlds": the object world and the world of consciousness. He sometimes feels that one or the other must yield priority. For the two worlds are in conflict; they do not seem to be of the same nature. Illusion seems to be at work either when a man "loses himself" in his daily work, or else when he imagines that his self is an alien in the daily world.

The difficulty is that just as we have no suitable language for talking about the self, so we have no suitable language for talking about God. Language borrowed from the object world is systematically misleading when applied to the self or to God. (The positivist, of course, experiences difficulties in both matters.) Nevertheless, language about God may have an empirical ground just as language about the self does; only it will have to be one step more indirect. Our awareness of our self is a criterion for the language we use about the self; by it, we can decide which predicates are more, which less, suitable for speaking of the self. Moreover, all language borrowed from the object world tempts us to conceive self-awareness by analogy with sense perception, even though self-awareness is not like sense perception. For first awareness is not a looking, nor a standing opposite to an object, nor even an introspecting of the self as an object. It is a consciousness, an alertness, to be attended to and reflected upon. And intelligent consciousness, too, follows in the pattern of awareness rather than in that of sense perception. When we come to speak about God, we must keep these observations in mind.

We cannot, in such brief compass, attempt a full-dress inquiry into the nature of God and the way in which each aspect of that nature might (however poorly) be spoken of. In every case, such an inquiry would tell us more about the limits of human understanding and human speech than about God. Nevertheless, human understanding as it were aims at God, fixes its sights toward him whom it never directly apprehends, and approaches toward him from many directions. Often we wish to say: "This cannot be God," and "That cannot be God"; the power and purity of our own intention do not allow us to credit certain alternatives. But as we advance toward spelling out our conclusions about God, led by our own theory about man's cognitional life (i.e., by our own self-knowledge), an analysis of what we wish to say about God must grow in complexity and technicality. A long and many-faceted tradition in philosophic thought can guide our reflections at various stages in their development; hardly an era of philosophical history has gone by in which new light has not been shed upon the path. But in our present philosophical climate, to speak of God's *nature* seems idle; for the question foremost in the minds of many is whether God exists at all: whether the alleged reality of God can in any way be related to human experience. Discussion of the nature of God would be largely wasted.

Nevertheless, at this stage of our inquiry a few points may perhaps be profitably made. I have no illusions about the fact that these next few pages will be among the most difficult and least satisfactory in this study; but it seems better to face the difficulties and broach the wide realm of discussion opened up by them than to pass the matter by in prudent silence. Guided in part by the Western philosophical tradition—more or less, but not specifically, Christian and colored often by a Platonic cognitional theory—let us raise certain questions about what God must be like. In no case will we be able to raise all the points which might be raised on each issue; but perhaps a general line of thought will emerge, and the shape of an underlying method become apparent.

There are two main guides which it seems wise to follow. Thus, first, we will not use any predicate about God that does not *at least* apply to ourselves as subjects. Secondly, we will heed the warning that language borrowed from the object world can mislead us into thinking that awareness is like sense perception, or that the "world" of subjects is an imitation of the world of objects. These guides do not carry us far enough; but let us reflect on them a little.

We must not think of God as having a body, or having senses: the attempt to imagine such a God leads to the ridiculous. If God knows, it cannot be in the manner of observing, measuring, testing; these are limitations imposed on the scientist by the conditions of human inquiry, which proceeds through the use of eyes, ears, hands, brain. A man is confined to a place, to a time, among objects whose laws of behavior he discovers through long, careful, physically wearying inquiry.

Science itself, of course, if not the scientist, escapes such confines. A difficult experiment for one generation is child's play for a later one. Thus intelligent consciousness admits of many degrees and modes. The man with mastery acts more surely, over a wider range, than the beginner. It is not man's painstaking accumulation of data, creating of hypotheses, or devising of experiments that offers us a model for God's mode of life. It is the experience of intelligent consciousness that "has arrived," that has gained mastery, that is complete. This experience, among men, admits of degrees and modes, and hence seems in principle subject to projection beyond human experience.

Such a projection may be licit. Anscombe and Geach, for example, in their little book *Three Philosophers*,[26] make the important point that in speaking of God we are using a general term, not a proper name. Such usage is not uncommon. They write: "The term 'helium' was first introduced to refer to an element that produced a certain line in the solar spectrum; but 'source of such-and-such a line in the solar spectrum' was not the definition of 'helium'; 'helium' was introduced as a new term . . . to refer to a material known only by inference not by examination of samples."[27] In the case of God, the general term refers to a mode of life "not to be found by observations *within* the world, like the life enjoyed by men or cats or cabbages."[28] We cannot answer directly what God's mode of life is like; at best, we can single out which things in the world he is not like, and which things he may be more like.

The chief virtue in taking intelligent consciousness as a model for conceiving of God is that it does not require a corporeal body for its referent. We have no direct experience of a conscious being who has no body. But consciousness (first awareness) is presupposed by all other experience, including sense-perception. Consciousness thus seems to be conceivable even in beings, if there are such, who do not share sense-perception. Intelligent consciousness appears to be conceivable as an articulation of first awareness, apart from sense experience. The requirement of a physical body and sense experience is proper to human consciousness, but does not seem to impose a necessary restriction on the modes of conscious life.

The acts of simple awareness and of insight, for example, seem conceivable apart from human agents. We cannot imagine what such agents would be like. Nor can we perform experiments that show, directly, what such agents would be like or whether such exist. But just as simple awareness is capable of more articulations than those of sense experience, and just as the leap of insight ("reasonable induction") exceeds the deliverances of sense data, so we may conceive of a subject who is capable of simple awareness and of insight, but who is not limited to operation through a sense organism. We appear to be able, for example, to conceive of a mind great enough to understand all of contemporary science. No one human mind can in fact contain all of contemporary science. The time required for a man discursively to master the requisite information, techniques, and insights exceeds any one man's length of days. On the other hand, the more of a genius a man is, the faster he appears to absorb information, learn techniques, and achieve insights. The greatest genius would be he whose processes operated with such scope and swiftness that his acts of knowing approximated a single act—a single sweep of insight. The discursiveness required by the limitations of sense, including sense-memory, would be at a minimum. At the limit, this capacity for consciousness and complete insight seems conceivable apart from a body.

Consciousness is not, for example, an activity which depends for its intelligibility upon corporeal visibility; the Invisible Man of H. G. Wells is perfectly intelligible. If we imagine that the Invisible Man also lacked corporeal resistance—could not punch nor be punched, only observe and speak—still, the concept is intelligible. The crux of the matter is that in order to be known *by us*, a conscious being must in some way make use of matter: speak to disturb the air waves, touch us, or in some other manner make himself known by material effects. The problem then becomes, how can an incorporeal being have corporeal effects? Must the laws of consciousness take precedence over those of matter? Can creative intelligence and will mold matter, within limits, as they choose?

By posing such problems, we show that we can move beyond our own experience, with our intelligence if not with our imagination. We can think such things, and approximate them in our own activities. By virtue of our own consciousness, we can understand the concept of a consciousness not confined to the object world, though we cannot picture such a consciousness. Any image we try to form of such a being is misleading, because it borrows the requirements of shape and size and effectiveness proper to the object world.

The emphasis in the concept "consciousness-without-body" is

not (negatively) on disembodiment, but rather (positively) on the activities of awareness and insight. This emphasis on activity derives from human experience. In moments of intellectual concentration, or again in moments of artistic contemplation or communion, we find ourselves "rapt," forgetful of the demands of our bodies, of the passage of time, of fatigue, of the need to eat. Such intense conscious experiences furnish us the direction in which total, unlimited, unconditioned consciousness is the upper limit. It is such consciousness that is our model.

Moreover, our experience in study, art, inquiry, reveals that intelligent consciousness is not a pale form of sensuous consciousness. It has its own proper intensity, and is more intense in some respects than sensuous consciousness. So also, consciousness-without-body is not to be conceived merely as an abstract ghostly awareness, lacking sensuous and intelligent consciousness. It is, positively, an awareness with an intensity of its own: instantaneous, direct, full, uninhibited by the restrictions of space and time. The mode of knowing proper to consciousness-without-body is to be conceived, therefore, as simple first awareness. The model is not the more complex, analytical second awareness. For such intense consciousness does not calculate, figure out, solve problems, reason. It is not a looking, as though it were an all-seeing eye, darting from one object to another. It is simply and restfully aware. Through our own lesser, ordinary first awareness, the model has a ground in our experience.

On such a model, God would know in the manner of first awareness. He is not a thought thinking himself as in the tradition of rationalist idealism. But he is conscious. He would not need to proceed through inquiry as we do. His awareness would be clear, instantaneous, and comprehensive. He would know rather in the manner of an expert, than like one who is just beginning an investigation. He would know, once and for all, all that science painstakingly has discovered and will discover, as well as those riddles of destiny affecting individual men that are not among the problems of science. His knowledge would not, like second awareness, be extroverted, analytic, propositional, self-conscious. It would be at ease, nonrationalistic, familiar, like first awareness.

Thus, our assertions exclude a great many predicates from language about God: he is not an object, nor is he adequately known in the manner of objects; nor does he know in the manner of a creature with body and senses. But do we know what we are saying when we say this? What is it like to be aware, without a body by which to receive stimuli? Exactly here the believer and the nonbeliever part company. At times, I find that I am content with this reasoning: (1) I am aware of a self unlike the objects around me. (2) God, at least, is more like me than he is like such objects. (3) The "world" of subjects in which God and I live is the more radically real; the world of objects passes. (4) Exactly what God is like, further than that he is not part of the object world and that he is at least as conscious as I, I do not know.

At other times, on the other hand, I am not so willing to leave the clear system, the solid pier, of the object world. I want to accept that passing world, in Sidney Hook's words, as man's "tragic estate."[29] At which moment am I more faithful to human experience?

Everything depends on how I interpret the human experience at stake. Sidney Hook, for example, is a dialectician for whom I have much admiration; but in this matter he fails to convince me. In the history of philosophy, his philosophic spirit seems most like that of the Latin Scholastics. Like them he attaches primary value to rational considerations of logic and language. "It may be," he admits, "that I am too literal-minded and old-fashioned, prepared to pay too high a price for clarity."[30] Among recent converts to Christianity, he notes on the other hand, ". . . it is not rational theology but mystical theology, not the principle of objectivity but of subjectivity, not the clear, if defective, arguments of Aquinas but the record of the tormented inner experience of Augustine, Pascal, Kierkegaard, which are found most appealing. To the extent that evidence is introduced it is drawn from feeling, the feeling of awe and sublimity, of holiness and humility, dogmatically interpreted as indisputable intimations of divinity. Reason is short-circuited by the assumption that there is a non-propositional truth about the nature of things, obscurely grasped in every intense experience."[31] Mr. Hook interprets subjectivity as basically emotive; he thinks it is grasped in the intensity of experience. He seems not to reflect upon the experience of first awareness that is at the base of every inquiry, nor the experience of the unlimited drive of inquiry, which raises questions about the justification of scientific, pragmatic, or any other intellectual method. It is in these experiences that intelligent subjectivity is active; such subjectivity is discovered, not in the emotions, but in the depths of intelligence. In these depths the subject decides the criteria by which it will recognize the claims of objects, and so criticizes itself in the light of its own intelligent first awareness.

Mr. Hook further thinks, following Feuerbach, that the predicates men attribute to God are "projections of human needs—not the needs of the understanding but the needs of the heart, not of the human mind but of human feeling: emotions, hopes, longings."[32] I think his accusation is too sweeping. The predicates some men attribute to God are, upon reflection, found to be derived, not from the heart or the feelings, but from their experience of intelligent subjectivity, and above all from the relentless and driving spirit of inquiry.

3. The Hidden God

The God whom we discover by intelligence does not break his silence, nor step forth from behind the veils. It remains easy to deny his presence. When we speak of him, we speak badly;

on every side, difficulties spring up thick and fast. Worse still, our speech about God is not based on direct experience of his presence. It must depend upon reflection on our own intelligent subjectivity. Only here, in reflection upon our own awareness and inquiry, do we stand at the threshold and become dimly aware of his presence; only here, indirectly and from a distance, do we catch a glimmering of whence it is inquiry arises and whither our intelligence is tending. "We would not seek God nor attempt to prove him if we had not already found him," Pascal has written. On the other hand, the glimmer of him that we detect is so vague, and the illusions it may be subject to so many, that many reflective persons will not lend it credence. Yet the glimmer is there, and we must struggle to make our language say precisely and well what it reveals.

"God is simply incomprehensible to any created intellect," a man who greatly trusted human intelligence has warned us. "Hence no creature can attain to a perfect way of knowing him . . . the names we impose signify after the fashion in which things fall under our knowledge. And since God is above our knowledge . . . names we impose do not signify in such a way as to conform to divine excellence, but only as they are measured by created things . . . Whatever can be thought or said of God falls short of him . . . because the names we impose signify in the way we understand."[33]

When we name God, we name him through our ability to note our own inability to name him in the ordinary fashion. We cannot point him out. We cannot devise a test by which certain observable effects will occur if there is, or is not, a God.[34] What we can do is note that our drive to understand is the source of all those other activities—pointing, describing, performing, and the like—by which we usually name things; and that it is also the source of the discovery that these methods do not suffice if we wish to name God. The source of our knowledge of God lies directly in the drive to understand. not in any of its limited activities. That is to say, our notion of God is not an exigence of any of our theories, our intellectual systems, or our pragmatic programs. We do not need God because he fulfills this or that conceptual or practical need. Our hunger for God is prior to our speculative systems and our practical arrangements. For it is founded in the unstructured, undetermined, unlimited drive to understand, which is prior to our inquiring and our doing.

Thus, if I am to express my belief in God accurately, I must emphasize that my God is not the last link in "the great chain of being." Neither is he the last explanation in a chain of explanations. He is the goal that is anticipated by my unlimited drive to understand. He is the one who puts a "chain of beings" or a "chain of explanations" in an intelligible context. He is not one among beings or explanations, not even the greatest, not even the supereminently greatest. For the things that we discover and the explanations that we verify are measured by our concrete inquiries. He is the one who makes inquiry itself intelligible. He is the source of the spirit of inquiry in men and of the intelligibility, such as it is, in things. If a joke has a point, a problem a solution, a mass of data a descriptive or an explanatory unity, it is because men can understand and jokes, problems, and data are understandable. The source of active understanding in man and of intelligibility in things is, in part, what I mean by "God."

In naming God, therefore, I "intend to name"[35] the one who responds to the *why* at the center of my intelligent subjectivity. He is not an explanation among explanations, but the explanation of why there are explanations. He is also, and much more importantly, the one whose friendship I may explore with unlimited mutuality; the one whose response to my unlimited drive to understand would be neither a complete speculative explanation nor a total pragmatic program, but the communion of an intelligent subject. For the hunger to understand is not only abstract, and not only pragmatic, but also personal: better to talk with a great scientist than to know him only through his theories; better to cooperate with a great statesman as a friend than merely to admire his work from afar. To come to understand fully is in some way to enter into a friendship, one intelligent subject in conversation with another.

It may be well to dwell on this point for a moment. Throughout this inquiry, we have slighted the role of friendship, love, and personal commerce in the furtherance of the drive to understand. Consequently, when we come to speak of God, we are apt to speak of him merely as the goal of our drive to understand —an impersonal "light," a "flooding intelligence," which makes luminous both our spirit of inquiry and the intelligibility of all those realities into which we inquire. Apart from such a God, the relationship between our spirit of inquiry and its cumulative successes in penetrating the intelligibility of the real seems arbitrary and merely fortuitous; that is to say, it seems radically unintelligible.

But human understanding is not impersonal; its base lies in intelligent subjectivity. The most self-critical response of human understanding to the world of which it is a part is the response, not of an impersonal intelligence, but of a human, intelligent person. It is quite possible that that personal response is vain and isolated; that it has been invited by no other Person; that it has no personal echo in the universe. It is quite possible that the universe is impersonal. But sometimes it does seem that those philosophers who believe the universe is impersonal support their belief by a cognitional theory which interprets human understanding impersonally. They have not come to grips with their own intelligent subjectivity; they interpret themselves in an impersonal manner; and thus they project upon the universe their own impersonality.

Inevitably, men understand the universe in terms of the cognitional theory by which they understand themselves. Those who understand the importance of intelligent subjectivity, friendship, and personal response in the ordinary development of intellectual consciousness are led to believe that the God who is in some way at the source of their own spirit of inquiry is also a person, not merely an impersonal intelligence. But what they mean by "person" is not "human person" in all respects, not "man writ large," not an idealization of man, not even a symbol of all man's moral and spiritual ideas. What they mean is an intelligent subject, creative (though not perhaps "the Creator," a notion proper to religious faith rather than to philosophy), communicative, the source of intelligence and intelligibility in men and in things. God is conceived not as a projection of man's ideals, but as the source of man's spirit and of the harsh world in which man finds himself: a person who is not a fantasy projected for man's comfort, but an Other whose reality brings the unrealistic man up short. As we do not well love our wives for what we wish they were but for their reality as they are, so our love for God as a person demands not wishful thinking but acceptance of the real. Still, philosophically, we do think of him as a person rather than as a merely impersonal intelligence, somewhat as we think of ourselves as persons rather than as mere impersonal intelligences.

It is important after this digression, however, to repeat the central claim we are making. We do not name God in the ordinary way, for he is not an object of our direct experience, nor an abstraction from our experience, nor a content to fill a conceptual role in our theories. In no way can we get our usual experiential and conceptual tools to take hold of God. When we name God, we name him by means of our own intentionality. We name him as the goal toward which our unlimited drive to understand is aimed. Thus, we name him whom we do not directly experience by means of something which we do experience, viz., our restless drive to understand. Moreover, we name him according to that part of our experience which enables us to reflect upon the limitations of our conceptual and experiential tools, and thus to stand in the presence of one who exceeds the range of those tools. God remains hidden. But those who are faithful to the drive to understand are able to spurn idols, discredit representations, turn away from illusions, detect fantasies and emotional projections, and, in short, maintain the intention of their entire subjectivity in accord with the drive to understand. They stand naked, helpless, but faithful in the presence of him whom they do not see. It is the sense of their own experiential and conceptual poverty, and their own fidelity to themselves, which leads them to silent adoration.

In Western history, God has been presented to us as one who is both near and far, so transcendent that we cannot represent him to ourselves in any picture or concept, and yet our friend. This double movement of transcendence and immanence makes sense to me, laden with conceptual problems as it is. If God is in some manner an intelligent subject, he can be both far and near; and I can be both utterly insignificant in the light-year histories of the galaxies and yet a friend of God. My knowledge of God derives from my own drive to understand. Whatever I can hope to understand, God surely understands. For he is, it seems, the one who makes understandable whatever can be understood. He is the spirit of intelligence who provides the context in which things can be related to one another and to human intelligence. He himself is not the collection of all the understandings man hungers to achieve; nor is he the answer to the last Why? that brings a halt to the regress of explanations. He is the one who makes possible the dialectical rhythm of inquiry and explanation, and the unity of all the understandings men can achieve. He is the intelligent subject of whom our intelligent subjectivity is a partial and finite echo, whose ways are not our ways, but whose activity and power makes intelligible the fact of intelligibility.

To ask "But who caused God?" is to have failed to reflect upon one's own drive to understand. It is to have confined one's attention to the regress of explanations that takes place in a system of concepts and propositions; it is to have conceived of God as an arbitrarily last answer in an essentially endless series. On the contrary, one must attend to the drive to understand, which produces such systems in profusion and is a priori limited to no one system. At the end of every finite inquiry, the drive to understand is self-authenticating; at a certain point, one decides that there is sufficient evidence to justify a claim. The drive to understand exceeds such finite claims, for it can then raise further questions. But the drive to understand also exceeds any and all infinite series of explanations. If, for example, one asks how explanation is possible at all, one raises a question that is not a member of that series. Of itself, the drive to understand is an exigence for the understanding of everything that is, including an understanding of why there should be such understanding.

Moreover, as the appetite of an intelligent subject, the drive to understand may anticipate that the response to this exigence is that of an intelligent subject in no way inferior to man in subjectivity or understanding. The hypothesis that fulfills this exigence, but exceeds man's conceptions, is that of a personal God. Whether or not there is such an intelligent subject is not here in question. The present point is that such an intelligent subject is conceived by reference to man's drive to understand, not to the products of that drive. God transcends all the products and contents of that understanding, in response to the dynamic *Why?* by which that understanding itself detects the limits of the finite. When all scientific and pragmatic questions are answered, man is still restless with inquiry. As man's intentionality outruns his concepts, so does his conception of God refer to his intentionality rather than to any conception produced by that intentionality. Our conception of God is like the aiming of a bow and arrow in his direction, when we know that any conception shot toward him would fall back to earth before it touched him. God is not, then, the last in a series of "causes" or "whys," for these are conceptions, answers to questions. He is the response not to any particular question, nor to the most general of questions, but to man's drive to understand in its purity and in its transcendence of the series of questions.

There is, however, a danger in conceiving of God as the transcendent, personal response to man's transcending, personal drive to understand. Some persons, particularly those inured to the categories of classical rationalism, take "understanding" itself to be a red-flag word. They think of understanding as a kind of seeing—of structures, or of the necessary connections between premises and conclusions, or of the link or overlap between concepts. And they take an appeal to the "drive to understand" to be a covert appeal to the classical intelligibility, order, and design of a world modern science has outgrown. Such an "understanding" and such a world view is not ours. For if contemporary scientists have come to understand that many events in our world do not occur systematically, but at random or statistically, they have done so by fidelity to understanding.[36] It is no small triumph of modern understanding to have invented methods for dealing with those events, or series of events, which to classical science exemplified the unintelligible. To reflect upon the fact that men sometimes understand, and that some men are driven by a hunger to understand everything that is understandable, is not to deny that in a universe of emergent probabilities[37] there are many surds, random occurrences, merely statistical laws, and many things of which understanding notes correctly that there is nothing to be understood.[38] To be faithful to the drive to understand is to respect the "irrational" as well as the "rational," and hence to live, not by the dogmas of the schools but by the reality which for man's intelligence exemplifies both intelligibility and unintelligibility.

To conceive of God as the transcendent response to our transcending drive to understand is not, then, to conceive of him as the God of classical rationalism, holding the universe in good order, sweet placidity, and logical design. On the contrary, it is to encounter the God of storms, disease, unrealized possibilities, dashed expectations, cruel deaths, and surds which mark a world of probabilities such as ours. As the one who responds to our drive to understand, he is not the principle of the irrational. But neither is he merely helpless in the face of it. At a later stage in our reflections, we must return to these issues. At present, it is important to break the hold over our minds still exercised by the habit of religious rationalism. God is no idealist, no romantic, no rationalist; he is real and his deeds bite with all the cruelty of the real. If we are to be faithful to the God discovered by human understanding, we must insist: God is cruel.

Yet it is a fact that some human beings ask questions of the universe in which they live as if there were an intelligent subject who understood their questions and responded to them, though in his own transcending fashion. It is not their loneliness, their alienation, their isolation that in the first instance is the motive-force of these questions; it is their drive to understand. Their fidelity to this drive does not blind them to the terrors of the God they seek.

Perhaps it is more mature to take this seeking for God as immature, the longing for a father or, in any case, a personal universe—a nostalgia that must be outgrown. Or perhaps it is more mature to trust one's own powers, and in spite of the fact that one cannot see God, nor understand the surds and evils of human life, to continue to be faithful to the drive to understand, from which flow many things that are beautiful and successful in the world.

In any case, for believer as for nonbeliever God remains hidden. No representation—as Edward Albee's splendid *Tiny Alice* dramatizes successfully—can mark a difference between belief and nonbelief. In the end there is between belief and unbelief a fateful similarity, a fateful ambiguity. The empty *nada* of the believer deprived of consolation is in the abstract virtually indistinguishable from the nothingness of the rigorous nonbeliever, who does not try to disguise from himself his own poverty.

Correspondingly, in behavior and mentality the compromising believer and the less than rigorous nonbeliever are quite alike: the borrowed religious values of the one and the practical atheism[39] of the other make them allies. Neither one is likely to understand naked belief, should they encounter it.

In this matter, Kierkegaard was surely right.[40] Religion is not for every man. It is a value, a skill, that can be acquired only at the expense of pain and blood. Many persons (especially those involved with institutional religion) are "tone-deaf" to true religion. They believe by convention, by conditioning, by emotion, by mutual support, by complacency. They drive from their midst those who have come to know the terrors of the living God, and who are thus too radical. God is not to be discovered through the ordinary experiences of human life, through ordinary conventions, through ordinary language; only pious feelings, "religious sentiments," acceptable words may be acquired by such means. Nor, on the other hand, is God to be discovered by the pragmatists, the philosophers, the scientists, whose decision has been made to explain God away, or to define themselves in such a way as to preclude the presence of God from breaking in upon their consciousness. Like the sun hidden by the clouds, God is perhaps no less present because they are not aware of him; and perhaps it is in his light that they go on understanding. A conversion of understanding concerning their own identity would be required before they could acquire skill in the matter of religion. For if one shares their state of mind, one simply cannot understand religion. From their point of view, religion has to be of such or such a nature; and once it is admitted to be of that nature it is trivial. Perhaps their point of view is correct. There is certainly much in the practice of religious people to confirm it.

It is an almost daily experience to meet persons who ask questions about the meaning of religion, but who could not possibly understand what one would like to say. Hence, one comes to think that human life is a matter of circles, or of levels. Those on some levels, in some circles, are simply incapable of belief. Their interests are wrongly directed. Their grasp of their own identity is wrongly placed. No use to speak to them of God. But the tables are, of course, just as easily turned: men convinced that to speak of God is to speak of a mythical Big Daddy, a useless and harmful waste of breath, cannot understand those who expend energy for religious purposes. Such interests seem misdirected. Believers' grasp of their own identity seems wrongly placed. No use to speak to them of the requirements of mature human life.

Let it stand, then, that God is equally hidden from believer and from nonbeliever. Believer and nonbeliever disagree on what it is to be a man. Attention to the drive to understand, its requirements and its implications, is the first step toward deciding the issue at its root. But the argument is not verbal. One must live for a certain little while in the alternative way of life if one wants to understand it well. Both ways of life can be lived, and nobly. The problem is to decide for oneself which way is most in accord with what it is to be a man, which, that is, is most in accord with the drive to understand.

To decide the question of horizon, the question of which perspective and sweep best suits the drive to understand, is to come one step closer to deciding the issue between belief and nonbelief. Neither belief nor nonbelief follows as a deductive consequence from this or that choice of horizon. But in some horizons the probabilities are higher than in others that through his drive to understand a man will come upon, and countenance, the reflections on human experience which give rise to the quest for God and ultimately lead him consciously into God's presence. It is therefore necessary to begin with questions of horizon, questions of intelligent subjectivity, in order to heighten the probability of our understanding, not to say of our resolving fairly and on its own proper ground, the issue between belief and nonbelief.

5 ❖

DECIDING WHETHER
TO BELIEVE

1. What Is Real?

Commonly, two reasons are given to explain why religious persons believe in God: they desire emotional security; they desire rational order. Religion is believed to originate in the feeling of emotional dependence, or in the eros of the necessary and the absolute. Yet neither of these reasons—which are not reasons at all, but only motives—is the reason for belief. For belief is rooted in the drive to understand. And understanding is neither emotional nor rational, neither emotive nor cognitive, in the sense in which these words are generally used in Anglo-American philosophy. A belief anchored in the hidden God does not bring emotional comfort, particularly in an intellectual climate that regards such belief as illusory. One's nonbelieving peers imply rather regularly that one is being dishonest, or at best lacks nerve. It is true, moreover, that God is silent; the moments of aridity and darkness are long; one does not see him in whom one believes. If belief brings "peace" or "emotional security," such peace is of a peculiar kind; and sometimes one would like to have some.

On the other hand, the drive to understand does not generate anticipations of rational order, necessity, cosmic harmony, or classical design. On the contrary, after a little experience, the drive to understand leads one to expect variety, many contingencies, an order that is often and at best statistical, probability schemes that perish in competition with other probability schemes in the evolution of human history. It leads one to expect surds and much that is unintelligible to men. One need not be a cosmic optimist, nor a rationalist, in order to believe in God. On the contrary, religious prophets often anticipate catastrophe, and the Christian symbol is the cross which involves a surd.

The decision to believe, made with authenticity, appears to have other roots than emotional weakness or monistic prepossessions. The decision to believe springs from a decision about what in human experience is to be taken as the criterion of the real. As each man is, so will he decide what is most real in human experience. According to that decision, he will shape his own identity. He will in ironic truth *realize* himself. An empty or a full life, nervousness or contentment, will later be the measure of his wisdom. It is a fascinating study to observe aging persons carefully, to see how they are reacting to choices made long years ago; or to observe the middle-aged, as they pass the crest of their accomplishments and begin to see, not what they will be when they mature, but what they have become. Sometimes there is suppressed terror, and sometimes peacefulness.

There are, commonly, many candidates for what is real in human experience. Nearly every person has at least three favorites: the one he speaks about conventionally, the one he cherishes as his serious conviction, and the one that reveals itself in his daily choices. These three are seldom unified. For some, "sincerity" is the most real of human experiences: sincerity regarding oneself and others, and the encounter with sincerity in others. But sincerity as a policy turns out to be an evasion of the basic question. For the basic question concerns what is real; and sincerity may or may not be based on what is real. If, for example, yesterday a woman told a man sincerely that she loved him, and today tells him with equal sincerity that she no longer loves him, she may not be being as sincere as she thinks she is. On the other hand, what she is being sincere about may be her present emotional state as it presents itself to her consciousness. But to be sincere about her present emotional state is only to be fickle. If what is most real to her are her present emotional states, the universe will, as it were, rotate on her as on an axis; and it is difficult to see how she will respond to other things or other persons as they are, rather than as they appear to her in her present emotional state.

The point is that emotional states can be recognized for what they are and discounted; there is no need for one to be imprisoned by one's moods of the moment, unless over the long run one likes it better that way.

Other persons may take "sense experience" to be most real to them. We may leave aside the problems of what exactly it is that sense experience presents to us—whether brute sense data, or whole physical objects, or *gestalt* configurations.[1] The radical question is how one is to interpret first awareness, insight, reflective judgment, and the drive to understand. For one appears to be drawing on all of these as one experiences, analyzes, argues, discovers, and justifies the fact that what appears to one's senses to be the case is in fact the case.[2]

Still other persons may take their own pragmatic purposes, or those of science or of the human community, to be the most real features of human experience: What counts is to realize oneself, succeed in a respectable career, be the best one can in one's profession, have good friends, eat well, and take steps through political and social action to maximize the numbers of those who can share in such good things. Then equality of opportunity, fair play, justice, war on ignorance and disease, reform of the political, social, economic, and familial order become the ideals by which one lives. But, on reflection, it appears that to devise such purposes, and to discriminate among purposes, one requires a vision of what man is. And to decide what man is, is to make use of first awareness, insight, critical judgment, and fidelity to the drive to understand.

What appears in fact, then, to be real to those pragmatic persons whose nobility in thought and action one cannot help admiring is what is in accordance with their fidelity to understanding. Pragmatism, as many Americans understand it, is not crass, small-minded, confined to what is expedient.[3] It is a policy of fidelity to intelligence, with emphasis on the requirement that intelligence be not idle but "make a difference" in the world. That is real which meets the demands of inquiring intelligence. If it were not for those contemplative moments of artistic creation and enjoyment, of reflection, of love, even of idleness and wonderment—moments which recur with an insistence that forbids their rejection as valueless—one would be inclined to uphold the emphasis on that part of intelligence which solves the problems of the world; and one would resolutely turn aside from mysteries that cannot be solved by reference solely to sense experience.

It is not pragmatism as such, but the confluence of pragmatism with a narrow form of British empiricism which cuts short inquiry about God. A larger pragmatism allows no such turning aside from mysteries. For there are moments when one becomes aware that one is different from the objects of the world; moments when one wonders that anything at all is; moments when one respects another person whom one loves, respects her as she is and not as one would like her to be, beyond any of the requirements of self-interest or self-aggrandizement, and even at some cost to one's own self-image, desires, or plans. There are also moments when one is struck by the unconscionable importance of individual human personality in the world in which we live, an importance that makes such categories as "role," "function," "usefulness" seem inadequate and demeaning. The world, at least the human world, is not accurately to be understood on the model of an ant heap, however humane, nor as a machine of production, however just and equalitarian in its rewards and opportunities. To be a person is to be inadequately provided for by models drawn from inanimate nature. In world views projected from such models, the human person is a stranger, an alien, an outsider. The human world, on the contrary, is personal, and requires a model based upon intelligent subjectivity if it is to be understood. To conceive of the world as the proper home of intelligent subjects, to reject analogies drawn from the mechanical uses of human reason, or the merely reflexive activities of the mind, may run counter to present prejudice, but it is plausible.

As we have seen, first awareness is the base of man's difference from other things in the world. This first awareness unfolds as the dynamism of inquiry; inquiry issues in understanding; and this understanding does not satisfy the drive of inquiry until it has been authenticated by critical reflection. If this description accurately expresses man's cognitional life (if not, it can be amended through a more accurate use of inquiry, experience, understanding, and reflection), then the real is that which is authenticated not by mere extroversion but by a complicated and lengthy inquiry. That is real for man which he attends to, inquires into, understands to the extent he can, and with sufficient reasons accepts to be as he understands it. Nothing is known to be simply because it appears or because it gives rise to an insight, for fantasies may do as much. That is known to be real which is apprehended by the understanding, and affirmed to be as it is by virtue of the reasons which support that affirmation. We do not know what is real until we have attended to the data, understood them, and supported our understanding with reasons that adequately withstand objections. The real is not what we touch, taste, see, and feel, but rather what we approve in our touching, tasting, seeing, and feeling, when we reflect upon the conditions under which our experience is taking place, our habitual successes and failures under such conditions, the present state of our sense organs, memory, and reflective powers.

What we affirm to be real when we say that a lamp is really out there in front of us is not that about the lamp which impresses our eyes and sense of touch.[4] It is that about the lamp which allows us to conclude that what impresses our eyes and our touch is intelligible as a lamp, and that what our eyes look at and our fingers touch is susceptible of inquiry and withstands reflection. Looking and touching enter into our verification of what is real; but looking can sometimes be merely "seeing things," and touches may sometimes be merely imagined. The real, then, is what is arrived at, not immediately by extroversion but mediately by reflection. The real is the intelligible, not in the first moment of understanding but in the second. It is that which is marked by the affirmation Yes to the question "Is that so?" Even among sensible things, the real is not what we look at or touch but what, with good reason, we claim to be seeing or touching, or to be able to see or touch if it were in our presence.

It seems, at first, odd to think of the real as the intelligible rather than as the tangible or the visible, especially when we are concerned with things as plain before our faces as lamps and rocks and trees. But reflection soon discovers the reason for this oddity. If I hold my hand in front of my face in perfect certainty that, in truth, my hand is in front of my face, one element in my certainty is my own first awareness; another is my sense of being awake and in at least normal spirits and self-possession. So it is not the case that what is known as real about my hand's being in front of my face is constituted by my seeing its brute, raw presence out there; what is known as real about it is constituted by a judgment authenticating my qualifications for seeing it there at the present moment, and its own qualifications for being seen. We protect ourselves from illusions, hallucinations, and fantasies by submitting to critical reflection what we appear to touch, see, or hear. The real is not known by simply touching, seeing, or hearing, but by understanding and verifying: the real is not the tangible but the intelligible.

Old-fashioned textbooks often counsel the awakening of a skeptic to reality by kicking him on the shins. Yet this technique is useful, not so much because it brings about the raw confrontation of toes and shins, but because it gives a start to the skeptic's awareness. It calls on him to retaliate; therefore to make a decision; therefore to come to terms with his understanding and critical assessment of what is happening; and therefore to begin a new policy of heeding sensory stimuli as intimations of realities that are not to be ignored, but understood. Sense-knowledge is not the most real nor the most certain of human experiences, but it is the most immediately provocative.

But if the real is the intelligible, then in being faithful to understanding one is being faithful to what is real. This fact seems to reveal why what we understand to be the case sometimes makes a claim on us which appears to be inescapable. We may fail to act according to our understanding, and we may seek refuge from it in the contrary opinion of others, or in rationalizations of our own; but sometimes the truth of our understanding is borne inescapably in upon us, and, despite our evasions, we recognize it as true. The real as intelligible, then, is not just a figment of our imagination, though we may try to escape it as though it were, and no one else may blame us. Sometimes it makes claims upon us whose strength an open mind quickly attests, which even an evading mind cannot wholly escape.

The real as intelligible is the product of a decision: a decision to accept as sufficient the reasons which support one's claim to know. Such a decision is made with reasons, not arbitrarily. Yet it need not be absolutely final, but merely a completed stage in an endless pursuit of the unconditioned. It is a decision that fulfills the conditions of the present moment of inquiry in the ongoing dynamism of the drive to understand. Further inquiry may call for revision in what is now taken to be real; yet those reasons which support the present claim, insofar as they are valid, will remain valid even in an extended or modified state of the question. Thus, development in knowledge has continuity, and the reasons supporting later stages include and subsume, as well as sometimes reverse, the reasons supporting early stages. There is a great deal of relativity in human knowing, since what one man decides are sufficient reasons for a claim to know may not be sufficient for another; and a later stage of human knowing may call for such serious revision of an earlier stage that some will be inclined to speak of "revolution," while others speak merely of "development."

The appeal, implicit or explicit, to first awareness, insight, critical judgment, and the dynamic drive of inquiry, however, remains constant in human knowing. And such an appeal constitutes human knowing as objective, not whimsical. It makes men the servants rather than the dictators of truth. Inquiry aims at what is real, not what is arbitrary; but the real is known only heuristically and partially: from a certain point of view, with certain purposes in view, within a given horizon or universe of inquiry.

The real, then, is the intelligible, and the dynamic drive of human intelligence is proportioned to it; that is to say, the universe in which we live seems to be such that within it fidelity to understanding is fruitful. When we are faithful to our drive to understand, we appear to act successfully, or at least more successfully than by any other program. For to try to determine what is real is to be prepared to act realistically. Faithful to understanding, a man appears to be more in harmony with other men and with things than in any other way; even love, apart from understanding, is destructive both of lover and beloved. Critical understanding is our access, limited as it is, to the real.

Unless these reflections are mistaken, to be faithful to understanding is in some way to be at home with other persons and with things; to cease being a stranger in the world; to end one's alienation. For understanding seems to be—in anticipation if not in realized fact—in harmony with the real. Our intentionality, unlimited and undetermined, appears to be one pole of a horizon of which the whole of the as yet unknown real appears to be the other. All that can be known as real is, by anticipation, present in the unstructured drive to understand; and the drive to understand hungers to understand all that can be understood. Even our capacity for sympathy with other persons can be extended beyond the bonds of family, history, and nation through appeal to a mutual drive to understand, a mutual fidelity to the demands of inquiry, a mutual respect for each other as each other is. Ideology demands conformity; but appeal to the drive to understand seeks community in diversity.

The real and the intelligible (the terms are convertible) appear to surround us, and to possess us rather than to be possessed by us. Through our senses and early experiences, the real is borne in upon our notice and, gradually, through our fledgling intelligence and knowing powers we appropriate it. Our minds are in some respects informed by the real as our lungs are stretched with air. Given a good start, we grow slowly in wisdom, detecting our own flights from the real, failing, and correcting our failures. Tragedy arises because we begin in ignorance, and yet cannot wait for wisdom before making choices and beginning to act. We are involved in unconscious patterns and surds in our actions before our understanding begins to be able to detect what we are doing. Struggling to come to self-knowledge, our lives have become dark and complicated beyond description before we are fairly under way.[5]

Still, our intelligence seeks the real as an arrow seeks its target; it intends to find, and to rest in, the real. We cannot be satisfied with illusions, nor with partial truths, nor with fantasies, except at the cost of diminishing our grasp of reality and inviting our own destruction. But when we follow this thirst for the real through to the end, does it lead us to God? It may be that the real ends where sense and imagination end; whatever cannot be reduced to corporeal sight or touch may not be real. The real may end where the uses of intelligence in the arts, the sciences, and the businesses of the world end. Belief in God may not be belief in the real, but belief in something beyond the real, and therefore, by definition, illusory.

We have not, however, acquiesced in the view that the real is the tangible or the visible. Quite apart from the question of God, this view does not seem to be tenable. The real is what, with reasons, we accept as intelligible and true to our experience. There is no other way of being united with the real; and the dynamic of inquiry, from experience to the first moment of understanding to the second moment of understanding, seems ineluctably to lead us in this way. It is difficult for many who are accustomed to think that they distinguish what is real from what is apparent merely by looking or by touching to agree that what is known as real is, not the tangible as tangible, but the tangible as intelligible. But reflection upon their own cognitional practice will show that not every sense experience is veridical, though, upon reflection, some are accepted as such.

The real, then, is reached through reflection; and what is real in things is that in them which withstands not only sensory exploration but also reflection. For we regularly discount appearances as deceptive or distorted because of departures from normal conditions, the refraction of light, an unusual distance or angle, the extraordinary condition of our own sense organs, or the like—departures which we recognize upon reflection.

If the real is the intelligible, then, it is not limited a priori to what we can experience with our senses. Our own intelligent subjectivity, for example, is not experienced through our senses, but rather the experience of our senses is possible because of our first awareness, and known to be veridical through inquiry and reflection.

Secondly, the unstructured drive to understand, by which we detect the limits of all our concepts and our rational systems, is not limited by what we can conceive or bracket in a rational system. The birth of a new theory, for example, is often first present in consciousness as a "glimmering," an expectation; sometimes only after long discursive effort is a new insight reduced to new concepts that can be related to familiar concepts, and a new rational system worked out to express it as the former could not. The drive to understand, since it is prior to concepts and systems, aims beyond them. At the limit, our unstructured drive to understand, then, does not merely anticipate a full, final concept or a rational system, a system to end all systems, in which the relations of every single event, or series of events, to every other is made clear. For the drive to understand is the appetite of an intelligent subject. When every scientific question has been answered, that drive will still seek another intelligent subject who responds to its anticipation of unlimited intelligence. Our drive to understand seems to be an exigence, not only for an understanding of all that can be understood but also for the source of such understanding and intelligibility. Its rest appears not to reside merely in an understanding of things, but also in intelligent dialogue with a person; not merely in seeing the point of theories, but in kinship of spirit with their authors. It will be well to recall several matters of ordinary experience.

The religious query seems to be a constant in human history. If our age is characterized by a widespread decision to declare the religious query illegitimate, it is possible that this decision arises from a preconception of what inquiry is, and of what is real. The quest for God is not eradicated; it is declared to lead off limits, and is ignored. "My soul," sings the Psalmist, "seeketh God as the hart panteth after water." In our generation, too, it seems true that many men seek God even though they have come upon no break in the wall by which to come into his presence, and even though that search is at present out of fashion.[6] Many others seem able to repress the question about God, and to live without suffering from his absence.

Yet not all are equally content in the belief that by such a choice they are doing justice to their drive to understand. For it does seem to be true that the drive to understand intends to reach the real, breaking through horizon after horizon in its effort to understand more accurately and fruitfully. And it is startling and repugnant to some minds to believe that an effort manifestly so fruitful and successful is out of harmony with the real; that is to say, is an accident, yielding no clue to the riddle of our destiny.

It would not be surprising that the universe were absurd. It would be surprising were there intelligent subjects who recognized it to be so, and yet seemed to be successful in coming to grips with it. Things seem to happen *as if* the real were the intelligible—not, surely, according to logical or classical expectations, but including surds and the unintelligible and the statistically probable in ways that men now detect. J. N. Findlay in defining his own atheism admits what he, with trepidation, calls a "god-ward trend" in things; "certainly there are *some* facts in our experience which are (one might say) *as if* there were a God."[7]

It is remarkable, for example, that men communicate with each other, form lasting and profound friendships, sometimes sacrifice themselves for one another, respect other persons quite differently from things, value creativity, build universities, and are incurably attracted by the ideal of fidelity to understanding. These facts are odd if the world of which these intelligent subjects are a part is radically absurd. It seems that in an absurd world there would be neither fruitfulness nor honor in being faithful to understanding. If the real is absurd, man's nobility doubles the absurdity by his failing to grasp the irrelevance of nobility and honesty. If man can *make* nobility and honesty relevant, the real is not quite so absurd as it seems.

If we observe what the nonbeliever does rather than what he says, we find that he acts as if understanding, friendship, honesty, nobility, and creativity are relevant to the real. If he believes that the real is without any meaning of its own, he creates his own values within it, as far as his power extends. But then his success at this project is a curious fact. Thus some nonbelievers appear to keep open the possibility of there being some sort of God, though they reject the conceptions of God they have encountered, and resolutely will not push their minds into the cold, unfamiliar darkness such an inquiry must brave. There is a strange fear of metaphysics in our generation, as though too many failures had broken our spirits.

Nevertheless, the finite answers to finite questions that preoccupy the workaday life of the scientist and the productive man do not exhaust the human drive to understand. For that drive, taken in its root and at its base, raises a different kind of question from any of those that occur in its ordinary problem-solving operations, in any of its efforts to predict and control. That question is whether the appetite of the intelligent subject is radically in harmony with the world, whether it is at home or in a strange land. The answer to that question is the first major step toward belief, or toward unbelief. For if the drive to understand is in harmony with the real, then the source of that drive and of the real may be one and the same. If the real is the intelligible, then there may well be a God.

Earlier, we came to think of God as the source of the intelligible and as an intelligent subject. These do not provide us with the content of a concept of God. For we do not understand what such a source, such a subject, might be like. But they do offer us a means of guiding what we may, and may not, properly say of God. Our earlier inquiry and our present one have now arrived at the same point: the real as the intelligible, God thought of as the source of the intelligible and of our intelligence, and our intelligence seeking its own identity.

Is there, then, a God? Have we evidence to support our belief that there is? It seems that we have one main line of evidence: all those things that seem to indicate that the real is the intelligible, and the insight which insists that, without an intelligent source, the intelligibility of the real is a mere accident and hence unintelligible. This, then, is the structure of the reflections that lead us to think belief in God is justified. The conviction that the real is intelligible, and the mere notion that God is both the source of the intelligible and the source of our intelligent subjectivity, lead us to *suppose* that that idea of God is true. Reflecting upon this supposition, and seeing its point, we conclude that there is a God, and that his existence and power explain why the real is intelligible, and why our drive to understand is as it is. This is the structure of the evidence and we will return to it in the next section.

Many, however, will choose to say at this point: "Yes, but the fact is that our science is only a more effective myth than, say, the Homeric myths;[8] we move from myth to myth; the world *itself* is simply unintelligible to us. And this is simply a hard fact to be swallowed by adults." They will add: "Yet the conclusion is not that we should despair. On the contrary, there are many tasks to keep us busy, and many incentives toward living a useful and satisfying life, without reference to a God we can in no way assure ourselves exists."

We may hasten to concede that "the world *itself*" is ever beyond our actual reach. But that our inquiries do not bring us to more effective and fruitful approximations of the real seems disproved by the success of those inquiries. We should not imagine that "world *itself*," or "objective," mean something out there now that we need to get a spiritual look at, in order to attain the real and the intelligible. Such a look is impossible. On the contrary, we need only detect that our drive to understand *seeks* the real, that the dynamism of inquiry heads toward the real, in order to say that the real is the intelligible. The "objective" is what in the context of reasonable discourse we are aiming at and what, at this stage in the heuristic dynamism, we now have good reasons to accept as fulfilling the conditions of critical inquiry. The "really, truly 'objective,' out there, independent of any human mind" is not accessible to us. It is appropriated only little by little, from approximation to approximation, as science develops and later inquiry corrects what earlier inquiry overlooked.

As to the incentives to be found for living "a useful and satisfying life," the decision for belief or unbelief appears to depend on one's threshold of satisfaction. Those satisfied by diversion and usefulness may choose one alternative; those in favor of trusting in their unrestricted drive to understand, beyond the limits of the conceptual, may choose the other. The key lies in who one is and what one expects from life; by belief or by unbelief one defines oneself. But it does seem that reflection on one's knowing activities favors belief. The exigence of our drive to understand does seem to be the intimation of the divine presence in us, the source of our restlessness, the occasion of our weariness with every finite diversion, every idol, every merely temporal achievement. One wants to be faithful to understanding quite totally—not to hold back for fear of the dark. Further, it sometimes seems as if unbelief represents a failure of nerve. One wonders what psychological pressures, what loves, what prior decisions, incline one toward unbelief, and away from fidelity to understanding, at the very moment when understanding makes its most basic claim.[9]

There are many reasons for unbelief—the problem of evil, the ugliness of religious organizations, rebellion against the injustices of a Christian civilization, conceptual difficulties, fears for personal autonomy, among others. But reflection upon our own cognitional activities seems to lead to the basic religious insight: the poverty of our own concepts and systems in the face of the exigence of our unlimited drive to understand. This drive seems to seek an intelligent subject, the source of the intelligibility of the real and the source of our own struggle toward the real. In that exigence we detect the invitation to believe, and thus to confer unity upon our inner life. For to respond Yes to this invitation confirms one's fidelity to understanding, reinforces it, and reconciles one to oneself, to others, and to the real. From the perspective of belief, so strong is this inner harmony, so clear the self-authentication of the drive to understand opening upon its fullest aims, that one cannot at first imagine a non-believer in harmony with himself.

On the other hand, one soon learns that fidelity to understanding is not a question of words. Many are faithful to understanding, yet do not believe in God. They refuse to reflect further on what it is to which they are faithful, perhaps because the name "God" has been cheapened on the lips of believers. The Jewish and Christian scriptures insist that God alone judges hearts and knows what is in man; our names are written in his sight, while we in the darkness grope to find out who we are.[10]

But since the God of believers cannot be seen, imagined, or conceived, the refusal of the nonbeliever to name such a God does not seem far removed from belief. The reality is more important than the words, and the reality in this case is fidelity to understanding. Believers and nonbelievers alike, faithful to this drive, appear to find harmony of spirit, a modicum of rest, and deep integrity.

2. Into the Presence of God

Time is required for the fact to sink deeply into our consciousness that the real is known through intelligent knowing rather than through mere sensory extroversion; through critical reflection rather than merely through taking a look. Once this simple and compelling lesson of reality is learned, however, the way to God is clearer and more straight. For if the real is the intelligible, two different lines of inquiry arise. One places the inquirer at the threshold of God's presence. The other prompts him to step forward into that presence.

The first line of inquiry is touched upon quite cautiously by

J. J. C. Smart in an essay whose title is "Can God's Existence Be Proved?"[11] Professor Smart's answer to the question expressed by his title is at least a tentative No. He considers the three post-Cartesian arguments as they have been listed by Kant: the ontological, the cosmological, and the teleological. He exposes with no uncertainty the fallacies in the conception of a "logically necessary being." He argues successfully that the way taken by intelligence to God is not that of "logical necessity"; and, with him, we may accept the fundamentally Kantian rejection of this way. But when he has finished with the useless concept of a "logically necessary being," Professor Smart initiates the sort of inquiry which seems to us much more fruitful. In the last paragraph of his essay, he raises the meditative question to which we have already seen Wittgenstein advert: "Why should anything exist at all?" At first, Professor Smart answers the question directly: "Logic seems to tell us that the only answer which is not absurd is to say, 'Why shouldn't it?'"[12] But then Professor Smart reflects further:

Nevertheless, though I know how any answers on the lines of the cosmological argument can be pulled to pieces by a correct logic, I still feel I want to go on asking the questions. Indeed, though logic has taught me to look at such a question with the gravest suspicion, my mind often seems to reel under the immense significance it seems to have for me. That anything should exist at all does seem to me a matter for the deepest awe. But whether other people feel this sort of awe, and whether they or I ought to is another question. I think we ought to. If so the question arises: If "Why should anything exist at all?" cannot be interpreted after the matter of the cosmological argument, that is, as an absurd request for the nonsensical postulation of a logically necessary being, what sort of question is it? What sort of question is this question "Why should anything exist at all?" All I can say is, that I do not yet know.[13]

Faced by the inquiry Professor Smart initiates so clearly, one may be inclined to think that the desire to continue raising the question of existence, and the awe which accompanies it, arise from the drive to understand. The reason we ask such a question seems to be our expectation, even if not articulated, that the real is the intelligible. It does not make sense to say that the real just happens; for then the real is radically unintelligible. It is an intelligibility whose source lacks intelligibility. Why should anything at all exist? Professor Smart thinks that the answer which is not absurd is "Why shouldn't it?" But, on the contrary, that is the one answer which does seem absurd. For to take the position "Why shouldn't it?" is to take the position "A reason for it is irrelevant; intelligence is out of place here; existence is simply not to be explained, but taken as a surd." Professor Smart's instincts are against this flight from understanding, and that seems to be why he is continuing his inquiry.

The search for a necessary being in rationalistic ontological categories, then, is hopelessly misleading; for this reason we may concur with the body of Professor Smart's essay. But when one comes up against the question "Why should anything at all exist?" and agrees that to say "Why shouldn't it?" is merely to evade, not to be faithful to, intelligence; and when one is fortified by the firmly critical awareness that the real is the intelligible; then one is brought up short before an awesome possibility: Perhaps the real has an intelligible source—indeed, an intelligent source. "Why should anything at all exist?" "Whence comes the real, which is all that is to be known?" In raising such questions, the threshold from which one may answer "God" has been reached.

Two meanings of "real" are then involved. There is the real which *raises* the question, "Why should the real exist?" There is, secondly, the real which is *intended by* the question: i.e., the intelligible and intelligent source which is an answer to the question. The gap between the two realities is immense. They are not consecutive links in a chain. They are as different as the data which raise the question and the answer that resolves it. They

are as related as the question requires. We do not need to have
caught sight of the intelligible and intelligent source in order to
agree that it is the source. It suffices to agree that the real is
radically intelligible, deriving from an unconceptualized but
intelligible and intelligent source. In agreeing to this one is not
bound to overlook the unintelligibles and the evils which also
characterize the real. These surds present a subsequent but
different dilemma: how can an intelligent source of a certain
kind—omnipotent and good—allow them?

A formal argument for the existence of God is not of much
use in the life of one who is trying to decide between belief and
unbelief. For what is at stake is one's recognition of one's own
identity, and there are many layers of point of view, inquiry,
and new horizon to come through before one can understand
the formal argument. Even so, to believe in God is not to accept
the conclusion of a deduction. It is to accept the evidence that
one discovers in one's own knowing and doing, indicating the
presence of a God who remains unseen and even unconceptualized. It is, above all, to enter into a conversation with that God,
not through words so much as through the direction of one's
attention. Thus, talk of the "intelligible" and "the real" and
"source," while indispensable as scaffolding, is not at the heart
of the matter. Only if each one who inquires appropriates the
way in which such words are being used, and laces it into his
experience, does the inquiry get beyond the scaffolding and the
poor words that serve as its signs. Only if those who share the
inquiry carry with them their experience, and steadily reflect
upon that experience, are they aware that what is at stake is not
skill in verbal gymnastics, but fidelity to understanding and,
through understanding, to experience.

At issue is an appreciation of the implications of our own drive
to understand and our appropriation of the real. These implications cannot be usefully schematized, because individual human
beings do not live by formal schemata. Each must travel the

circles of self-discovery for himself, by those steep paths along which fidelity to understanding leads him. To begin such a search is already to have found God, even though the seeker, looking for an object—something to see—does not notice him. As Pascal suggests, to seek God is to be faithful to that drive to understand which has him for its final goal, and thus, in a significant way, is already to have found him. Even the believer can do no more than point toward a God whom he cannot see.

If we think of God, then, as the source of the intelligible, such as it is, and as the source of our intelligent subjectivity, then, if there is a God, the intelligibility of the real and our ability to know the real are related in their source. If our experience seems to indicate that the real is the intelligible—that fidelity to understanding, friendship, love, creativity, nobility, are relevant to the real world in which we live—then we seem to have found an indication that there is a God. For if there is a God, fidelity to understanding is not an ironic or a desperate or a Promethean way of life; it is the realistic way of life. The world may be cruel as well as beautiful, full of risks as well as comforts, the unintelligible as well as the intelligible, and of evil as well as good; but man is at home in it, at home as a pilgrim, perhaps, but not absurd, not isolated.

If, on the other hand, there is not a God, then the intelligible just happens; it is of itself unintelligible. And the fact that men can make realistic judgments, both in their knowing and in their doing, is an oddity. Every appeal to intelligence also makes an appeal to the drive to understand, to its intention of reaching the real, and to its competence in dealing with the real. It does not seem plausible that man's intelligence has no intelligible relation to the real, that it struggles for effectiveness in a world that is not susceptible of being dealt with by intelligence. Further, it seems implausible, though not impossible, that the real is indeed intelligible but it "just happens" to be so. One cannot bring oneself to see that there is a God by induction, or by deduction.

One can only bring oneself to see, by reflection, what a consistent and thorough fidelity to understanding seems to indicate: (1) that understanding is not impotent in dealing with the world; and (2) that our understanding anticipates an intelligent subject as the source of its own drive to understand, and as the source of that drive's success in coping with the world.

Belief in God is rooted in reflection upon one's own intelligent subjectivity. But such reflection is not compelling, since not all men understand their own identity in the same way. It is only compelling in the sense that either fidelity to understanding operates "in the teeth of" the inscrutability and absurdity of the world, or it is a sign of the world's own intelligible dynamic. Much then, depends on one's spontaneous or acquired confidence in fidelity to understanding—as against, let us say, analogies from physics or mechanics—as a key to understanding the world. The drive to understand, it seems, points to God; we do not succeed in efforts to train our senses, imagination, or even concepts on him. To trust that pointing, or not to, is the question.[14] Some who habitually live by understanding, who struggle to move from horizon to horizon toward the real, will be inclined to credit understanding.

The second line of inquiry leads to this goal in a different way. Again it is required that one have come to see, implicitly or explicitly, that the real is not what is touched, seen, or heard, but what is understood and, on reflection, verified. A dagger in the air, a sound in the night, the touch of a mosquito on one's leg in the darkness, may be seen, heard, or felt, but they may or may not be understood and verified as real. What is touched, seen, or heard is at best a question for reflective intelligence, not a guarantee of what is real.[15]

Moreover, it is required that one reflect upon the dynamic movement of one's own act of understanding. For it occurs to some men that the finite things that they come to accept as real, the finite theories that they accept as true, and even the whole system of their common sense and scientific judgments do not exhaust their drive to understand. The more they reflect upon that drive to understand, the more they are led to wonder what, exactly, would respond to it and give it the full activity of rest. In this light, every finite proposal, and every extension of the finite to the infinite, seems inadequate. No one finite object, nor any infinite series of finite objects, offers to do more than to divert them, keep them occupied, and, finally, bore them. Moreover, the drive to understand is the appetite of an intelligent subject. There is a possibility that the full response to this drive is that of another intelligent subject. On such a supposition, the world in which we live is radically personal. A subject who responds to our intelligent subjectivity, as abyss cries out to abyss, would then be the source of the intelligibility of things, and also the source of that communication which in fact takes place between persons, through art, friendship, love, justice, rational discourse. On such a supposition, the world of human experience is not only, in spite of its appearance, "a bump on a bump"[16]—a tiny edge of consciousness on a tiny edge of animate life in a vast universe—but also the interpretive key to the rest.

One need not, in this supposition, assume that the divine is in the form of a man, or bounded by human limitations. One need only suppose that he is known indirectly by the unlimited, searching drive of our own intelligent subjectivity, and its rejection of all lesser objects offered in place of him. He is the response to our thirst for unlimited intelligibility and personal dialogue. Exactly what he is like, we need not and cannot imagine. Yet our approach to him is critical, since it proceeds through reflection upon our own unlimited drive to understand. Fidelity to that drive is necessary and sufficient for the rejection of idols, the correction of fanaticism, and respect for the human person, in oneself and in others.

To entertain the reflection that everything exists for reasons and in a manner known by an intelligible and intelligent source, or to think that finite objects do not exhaust the questions raised by our own nature, is not yet to have entered into con-

versation with God. It is only to have come to the threshold of
his presence. At this threshold, for various reasons, many will turn
back. The intellectual air here is too thin. There are enough
things to do in our cities, our governments, our underdeveloped
economies and health centers and schools, without opening such
a difficult and energy-consuming line of inquiry.

But some men will think it in accord with their own identity to
press further. Some will think that man is as naturally religious as
he is social, political, economic, or artistic. Moreover, the religious sense is a sense that needs effort, practice, and exploration
like any other. Its base lies in the unlimited drive to understand
and it has the real for its horizon, so it requires the disciplining
and harmony of all our other powers.

The step into God's presence is achieved in a fashion that can
be described, but not accompanied by detailed instructions. One
comes to trust one's own drive to understand. Then, quite simply,
one begins to speak, even though God is hidden. If one's preceding reflections are correct, one stands already in his presence.
Special words are not required; one can be speechless. For he
knows us from before we were made; he knows our thoughts
before we form them. Those infidelities to understanding that
have escaped our attention have not escaped his. Far from destroying our drive to understand, or bending it down to the earth, he
requires us to be more faithful than our own standards have yet
insisted. He impels us toward more demanding honesty, more
singular courage, more independence of our cultural milieu, a
greater sense of community with other men who are caught in
the same night, than we have yet practiced.

The terrifying thing about the discovery of God is that one
comes to see that he has been there all the time. He is not dead;
we have been dead. Even believers who neglect him, mumbling
routinely through their prayers, will one day come upon this
terror. To meet God face to face—quietly, wordlessly, wholly
attentive—is no comforting experience. Moreover, the way in
which this sense of the holy, of awe, of dependence, is described

in books is partly misleading. For the uninitiated will think of the brute awe of standing before the Grand Canyon, or high in the cold Alps, or of the emotional dependence of the immature boy upon his mother or the dependence of his superego upon his father. But the encounter with God—with the living God and no counterfeit—is a chastizing experience. For it is accomplished not in the context of warm self-satisfying illusion, but in the nakedness of the self's critical drive to understand. In that light, one's inadequacies are only too plain. Standing in that light, nonetheless, one has the dignity of attempting to be faithful to oneself. One offers God one's ardent efforts to be honest. God is hidden, the self is naked and impecunious, but in this scorching light it is good to live.

Having entered God's presence, moreover, I cannot accurately say that I "possess God" or "have belief." It seems, rather, that God possesses me, that belief has surrounded me. This difference does not imply a loss of one's bearings, a mystical flight, a sense of being suspended in air. It merely represents what seems then to be the case, viz., that the dialogue between oneself and God is not initiated by the self; that when one is faithful to understanding one is responding to an attraction in the core of one's subjectivity; that God has done the calling, the guiding, the leading, and made it possible for men to respond, to be guided, to be led. It is not, however, as if God is separate from me and takes over my autonomy as a writer takes over a pen, or an artist a brush. It is rather that my autonomy, my separateness from things and from others, my full measure of responsibility to myself, my *own* drive to understand and commitment to my *own* understanding, are the very things that God respects, the very things through which alone I can authentically find him.

In possessing me, God does not dispossess me of myself; he invites me and he respects my response. He does not ask me to abandon my autonomy, lest he leave me with nothing to offer him, and no way to find him. But I know with clear instinct that in being faithful to my own identity, I am faithful to him. In being intelligent, I am living by the light of his intelligence. In feeling the bite of objective honesty about myself, I hear his word. In respecting other persons, in loving them realistically, as they are, I do as he does. In creating, I share his fecundity. In him, it appears, I live, move, and have my being.

Yet is this nonsense and a myth? Perhaps. Not seeing God, one cannot help doubting, and worrying about conceptual difficulties. The hardened nonbeliever, who has considered a score of arguments, digested hundreds of books, and uncovered a thousand religious hypocrisies, will turn the skills of analysis upon such reflections as these. Sometimes he will almost convince me entirely, and always he will convince me in part. The drive to understand seeks relentlessly for intelligibility, and indeed for the response of an infinitely intelligent subject. Perhaps it does so in vain. But when I trust fidelity to understanding in my scientific work, in my writing, in my moral efforts, in my friendships and my loves, I am loath to distrust it in facing the riddle of existence. Understanding occurs. Love occurs. Respect for persons, and also friendships, occur. I am inclined to think that these are the significant occurrences in the universe, that, whatever the ravages of the unintelligible and the positively evil, these characterize the real, and that whoever trusts in understanding and in love is in harmony with the real. The God of intelligence and love draws men toward greater understanding, greater love. The dynamism of human development, however infinitesimal in the perspective of the universe, is the clue to the presence of God.

Nevertheless, children starve to death, and men of understanding and love are pointlessly murdered. Organized religion has often been the protector of an unjust social order. Conventional religion is largely false, delusive, and crippling. These are the reasons that most draw me toward unbelief. Reflection upon my own identity draws me toward belief.

6.

GOD OR EVIL

1. The Irrational

No argument against belief, however, is so cogent as the argument from the power of evil in the world. The fact of evil is overpoweringly present: Auschwitz and Belsen, the girl of thirteen struck by an auto, the boy of eleven whose face is corrupted by cancer, eighty children burned to death in a school, the thousands of the world's poor who starve to death each week. The believer insists that God is good and that God is omnipotent and omniscient. God knows what will happen, and he can act to prevent it. An earthly father may be frantic to save his boy's life; the heavenly father seems to do nothing; the boy dies in great pain. It seems obvious that God is either not good or not omnipotent; obvious that he cannot be both.

If God is evil, or if there is no God, the problem disappears. If God is evil, the believer has no argument with the nonbeliever; both are free to despise God. If there is no God, man takes his chances with a blind fortune. The issue only arises, then, because the believer insists that there is a God and that he is good. But the evils so manifest in human life tempt the believer to think there can be no such God; and the nonbeliever has already accepted that conclusion.

In his usual clear fashion, Henry David Aiken offers us a nonbeliever's statement of the problem in his essay "God and Evil." Mr. Aiken takes theological utterances at their face value, though with neutrality and fairness. His present statement is based on Philo's formulation in Part X of Hume's *Dialogue*; it represents fairly the tradition of the Anglo-American non-believer:

> By hypothesis, an almighty and omniscient being can do whatever it wills. But any perfectly good person, so far as he can, will do good and prevent evil. Now, if there is a being that is at once almighty, omniscient, and perfectly good, it will be both able and willing to prevent evil. On the other hand, if something is evil, it must be concluded that there is no such being, since a perfectly good person would prevent it if he could, and an almighty and omniscient being could prevent it if he would. Either, then, there is no such being or nothing is evil. But since, by hypothesis, only such a being is God, we are forced to conclude either that there is no God or else that there is nothing which is evil.[1]

Mr. Aiken's argument rests on a conception of God that is anthropomorphic in a special way; but it represents, probably, the way many people think of God. From the point of view of philosophical understanding, however, the crucial issue is how we are to understand the key words "omniscient," "omnipotent," "person," "moral agent," and "good," when (1) we use them of man, and when (2) we use them of God. If we think that the key terms are to be used in the same way for God as for man, as Mr. Aiken appears to think, then manifestly God does not measure up to human standards; he is cruel, sadistic, or simply nonexistent. But if our understanding of the key terms does not lead us to use them in the same way for God as for man, what, then, do we mean when we use these terms? How can we use ordinary words in extraordinary ways?

The difficulty is not, then, as Mr. Aiken avers, that of finding excuses for God or of justifying God's ways to man.[2] The difficulty is to find an adequate conception of God. In order to discover what God must be like to do as he does, one must do justice *both* to the facts of evil and to the nature of God. The crucial question is, What kind of agent is God? What is his relation to human history? Mr. Aiken's conception of God is the weak link in his analysis; his God is supposed to be good as man is good. On the other hand, Mr. Aiken does reach a conception of God which is at least more sophisticated than that of some fundamentalists. He sees that by saying God is omniscient we do not commit ourselves to saying that he would know how to square the circle. "On the contrary, [he] would know with blinding clarity that the circle cannot be squared."[3] Again: "Just as Omnipotence is not expected by sensible men to do the impossible, so Omniscience is not expected to know more about the impossible than that it is such."[4] Mr. Aiken also sees that "in asserting that there is an almighty or omnipotent being one is saying that there is something whose nature it is to act and whose power is unrestricted."[5] Mr. Aiken recognizes that logical difficulties can be brought against conceptions of omnipotence and omniscience. But he is willing to grant that terms long used in certain contexts acquire a meaning which, we will usually find, "is neither vacuous nor inconsistent."[6] He is able, then, to move within the context of religious language to decide what such language means.

It is indispensable to have a model by which to understand such language. Mr. Aiken's model appears to be man as moral agent. It would appear to be impossible, he writes, "to speak of an almighty and omniscient being as a good person without in some degree treating it as a moral agent and hence as, in principle, subject to the blame to which moral agents are liable."[7] To place God beyond good and evil, beyond praise or blame, is to relieve him of important attributes of personality.[8] Mr. Aiken warns against the tendency, which he discerns in Kierkegaard and in Buber, to make God transcendent in absolute holiness, while the effects of his moral personality in history—his law, his justice—are impugned as cruel and senseless. Mr. Aiken wishes God to be judged by the same standards as men, lest God become irrelevant to man's moral striving.

Kierkegaard might reply that Mr. Aiken is still viewing the

world on the plane of the ethical, and has not yet begun to understand religion. Kierkegaard, in short, might turn Mr. Aiken's standards upside-down and judge man by God's standards, not God by man's. Mr. Aiken's argument might in this light represent the quintessential attitudes of the nonbeliever: God is measured to man's cloth. On the other hand, we have assumed throughout our inquiry that the decision between belief and unbelief is not, finally, a matter of a blind leap, nor of personal inclination, nor of education in a different tradition; nor is it a matter of proof. Belief is born of a decision, supported by intelligent and critical reasons. Moreover, as Mr. Aiken emphasizes,[9] this decision is central to the way we live our lives; it is not idle sport, it has effects. So it is not enough for believer and unbeliever each to ask the other to adopt a new point of view. What reasons can be assembled for adopting one vantage point rather than the other?

The fact of evil cuts the believer's faith very deeply, and strengthens the intellectual certainty of the nonbeliever, because it seems to indicate that concerning God reasoning is useless: God's actions are neither rational nor moral in the sense in which we generally use these terms. And if we call a dispensation that allows millions of persons, through no fault of their own, to starve to death or to be decimated by plague "rational" and "moral," then our use of these words seems idiosyncratic. For a man who condemned others to starvation or disease would normally be thought of as "irrational," and what we call "moral" in the practice of God would, in the practice of a man, be called "immoral."[10] It is possible to argue, of course, that different standards of values apply for God and for man. God is graded[11] "good" on one scale, man on another, and the two scales are not commensurate. There is a "higher wisdom," a "higher good," which God in every case brings to fruition in a way mortals do not understand. But in that case God is not what ordinary people appear to think he is. His benevolence may be what among ourselves we call cruelty. His loving-kindness may seem, in a human frame of reference, sadistic. God is terrible as well as merciful. He crushes men with blind power, as well as calls them friends. Religion appears to be double-talk, and the effort spent justifying God's ways to man seems to be merely an escape from man's real difficulties and necessities.

On the other hand, a reading of the Book of Psalms, for example, does teach believers to weigh God and man in different scales, and to approach God as one who is holy, terrifying, and powerful, as well as gentle, loving, and considerate. It is not that God "has moods"; it is that he transcends our scale of values. It is not that he is arbitrary; it is that he alone sees the intelligibility of what he does. But what, then, is to make God's judgments relevant to our judgments, his morality relevant to our morality? There seem, at first, to be two alternatives: We can serve God; or we can serve man. We can attend to God's commandments, known to primitive peoples through his epiphanies in nature and the taboos of their culture, and to later peoples through revelations. Or we can try to use our own intelligence and courage, to make this earth more habitable and life on it more just and peaceable. The choice seems to be between an irrelevant religion and an effective secular morality. If we imitate God, we accept poverty, ignorance, and disease as part of the natural order; if we love man, we work to diminish the amount of suffering in the world.

But the alternative breaks down at a crucial point: it depends on the origin of our conception of God. A concept of God developed within the framework of classical rationalism may, according to the conventional beliefs of middle-class morality, postulate a God of "order and design," a God content in his heaven and rewarding his own on earth, even a God of liberal progress. In reaction against this God, the truly religious will flee to the transcendent, mysterious God who makes his own suffer and proves those he loves by ways men do not fathom.

The irreligious will object to the patent falsity of the middle-class God, and to the irrelevance of the orthodox God: if God is so transcendent, human distinctions—between democracy and Nazism, for example—are meaningless to him.

The dilemma of the "post-Christian" age seems to lie in the concept of God favored in the "Christian" age. It was for this reason that we tried to be careful in analyzing our concept of God, to refer it not to the conceptualizing intellect, the desire for order, logic, and design, but to the prior dynamism of the drive to understand. Our concept of God is not, properly, a concept of God; we do not pretend to know what he is. It is a projection from the intentionality of our native intelligence, the unstructured appetite for understanding. We were also careful to point out that our drive for understanding is quite capable of recognizing surds as surds and the irrational as irrational. For the intelligible that our intelligence appears to seek is not the fanciful, the logical, or the sentimental, but the real. The God who is anticipated by such a drive to understand is the God not of the fanciful, the logical, the sentimental, but the real.

This shift in the way we conceive of God suggests a shift in the way we conceive of the problem of evil. We are not surprised that there are evils in the world; the existence of evil is a fact. Nor does the fact of evil in the world stand athwart our affirmation that for the real to be the intelligible, there must be a God. For the real includes evil; and though evil is a surd, still, we can know it as a surd and so, as if inversely, account for it within our knowledge of the real. The God in whose existence we come to believe is the God of the real evil-ridden world, not the God of a world without evil. Our new problem of evil is how to relate the God of the drive to understand to the surds of actual history. We do not begin outside the actual, historical world, in a world of order, design, and logic such as never has existed. We do not try to discover how a God of order, design, and logic could have become involved in the irrational. We begin with the real, and we accept the fact that God has willed the real to be what it is. We do not ask why he so willed it, for we do not pretend to have insight into all possible worlds, nor to stand in judgment upon God. We are not trying to justify God. We are trying to understand more clearly, from the fact of evil, what he must be like in order still to be called good. We are seeking a more profound understanding of who God is. We seek it, not for his sake, but to assure ourselves that it is no monster we worship.

The dialectical significance of the problem of evil, seen in this light, is that it makes men seek the true God and no counterfeit. When men do not feel the bite of evil, they regularly make God over in the image of their own comforts and conventions, and are content to think of him as benevolent, reasonable, tractable; they domesticate him. It is the fact of evil that makes us seek out ruthlessly and clearly who he is in whom our belief is placed. Evil is the school in which we are made to put away the God of childhood.

But the philosophical significance of the problem of evil is the light it sheds on the meaning of good. For if the God replacing the God of childhood is both omnipotent and good, our notion of good requires as much deepening as does our notion of God.

2. The Good God

It is a radical mistake to pose the problem of evil in such a way that we view ourselves as morally superior to God. We might say, for example: "Since God is omnipotent, why didn't he create a better world than this one?" We are not called to pass judgment upon God, however, nor to assume a privileged access to God's mind, so as to ascertain his motives for choosing the present dispensation. Our task is much more sensible. It is to try to understand if the fact of evil indicates that the way in which God is good requires us to modify our criteria of what is good. For belief in God, if more than verbal, has effects. And belief in different kinds of gods may be expected to have different kinds of effects. Since God is usually conceived of as some sort of moral judge, one set of such effects concerns our notion of the good.

The problem of how to define "good" has troubled English philosophers for some years.[12] In their little book *Three Philosophers*, Anscombe and Geach handily summarize the three theories which seem current in contemporary English philosophy:

(i) an identification of goodness, by definition, with some particular good-making attribute (theories of this sort are said by their opponents to exemplify the "naturalistic fallacy");
(ii) the view that the adjective "good" in its primary acception has a commendatory or prescriptive, not descriptive, force;
(iii) a view that goodness is an odd "non-natural" attribute, united by a queer (non-logical and non-causal) "must" to the good-making characteristic.[13]

Geach and Anscombe then point out that there is at least one more alternative known in the history of philosophy. According to this alternative, goodness is not identified with any one good-making attribute. Rather, for every good thing there is a good-making attribute such that for *that* thing to have that attribute is to be good. "There is no multiple of a number that is always the square of the number; but for any given number you can find a multiple of it that is its square—the double for 2, the quadruple for 4, and so on."[14] Thus "good" is not devoid of descriptive force, even though there is not one attribute common to every application of the word. Each thing has its own goodness, a quality, a disposition, or the like, whose absence mars the thing, whose presence makes it good.

The flexibility of this approach recommends it; it seems to be a *good* approach. What, then, is man's special good-making attribute? To answer this question intelligently, for himself, each man would first have to know his own identity. How will he know what makes him good unless he knows who he is? To answer the question of good, it appears, a man must appeal to the dynamism of intelligent subjectivity. It may then seem, for example, that the primary good for man is to be faithful to the drive to understand in trying to understand himself. For if he miscalculates concerning his own identity, he will achieve the good for him only by chance, not by choice. Men seem often to taste regret for precisely such miscalculations.

Fidelity to understanding, moreover, appears to be a useful proposal as a candidate for what makes a man good. For it is a criterion proper to each man individually, so that men are not pressed into one mold. Secondly, it is a criterion to which men seem to appeal spontaneously, even when they fail to live up to it; for, commonly, men who live according to convenience, comfort, impulse, whim, ambition, or other estimates of what is good rationalize their choice. It is, to paraphrase Lord Russell, open to men to live like pigs if they choose. But what is not open to them, without appealing to the dynamism of inquiry, is to justify that choice. When a man begins to justify the way he lives, he appeals to the criterion of intelligent subjectivity and, specifically, to fidelity to his drive to understand. His justification may apply to no other but himself, for no one else may be quite like him or in quite his circumstances; thus the criterion of good for him may be quite concrete, determined, and nuanced. On the other hand, if he is faithful to the claims of understanding, others will be able to recognize his choice as good if only for him; thus the criterion is susceptible of public inquiry. We do not usually recognize our failings, in fact, by introspection but by intersubjective criticism and discussion.[15]

Fidelity to understanding, therefore, meets both the requirements which a serviceable criterion of man's good must meet. It is personal to each man, yet subject to the scrutiny and questioning of all.

Thus, as a *method*, it is useful to all men of all times and in all circumstances; in this sense, it is generalizable, and an individual's use of the method in a concrete case can be criticized in detail. A general *maxim*, moreover, or a *proposition* in general form, is not nearly so applicable in particular, concrete, and contingent circumstances as is this method. For a generalization or a universal is bound to suffer from inadequacy in certain situations. But the policy of fidelity to understanding, from which generalizations and universals spring in the first place, requires intelligent attention to *every* situation in its uniqueness.

Finally, this method is objective, in the sense that any decision made in accordance with it can properly be subjected to interpersonal and even public criticism; and if this criticism convinces a man faithful to understanding that his own decision is wrong, he would be obliged to correct it, or if correction comes too late, to repent it. The man faithful to understanding, then, is the man of single eye, pure of heart, whose instinct for correct ethical judgment withstands scrutiny. His heart may lead his head, but only because his heart is already fixed upon fidelity to understanding before concrete and contingent situations arise.[16] To be such a man is to be a good man, and to be such a man at least by repeated effort if not by steady attainment is to be trying to be good: to have chosen the policy of the examined life which is, of all lives, worth living. Strictly, no other policy of life is justifiable. As hypocrisy pays tribute to honesty, so does rationalization to fidelity to understanding.

But there is something more important still about the policy of fidelity to understanding as the policy of the good life. As the drive to understand is objective and leads beyond the interests, utilities, and biases of the subject; and as the drive to understand is ultimately an exigence for the transcendent intelligent subject, God; so man's good appears to transcend the interests, utilities, and biases of the subject, and to reside in God. To have gained union with God is to have satisfied the profoundest hunger of the human spirit. To have gained God and to have lost all else is still to have remained faithful to the drive to understand, and to have preferred what is best to all that is good.

Moreover, no evil can take this divine good away from us; we lose it only by our own choice, by deliberately fixing our affections elsewhere. For we are free to fix our affections elsewhere for whatever gain may appear to be in it: logical, scientific, moral, sensitive, or emotional. But it is difficult to see what is to be gained by fixing upon less basic appetites, while renouncing the radical appetite of intelligent subjectivity, from which the others derive what critical light they possess.

The good for man, then, is, in general, the policy which is decided upon through fidelity to the claims of understanding; in particular concrete cases, the course that the man faithful to understanding would choose; and, ultimately, the objective of his drive to understand, that intelligent subject who is the source of the real, the God aimed at in every realistic, intelligent policy and every realistic, intelligent decision.[17]

Suppose, for example, we take God to be the source of the emerging intelligibility of a world process not yet at term, a world moving through countless series of probabilities from one threshold of realization to another.[18] Then, to choose a wise policy or to make a wise decision is to contribute by that much to the intelligibility and to the fruitful reality of the evolutionary process. It is to be creative, and hence to be like God. To choose a policy which runs counter to understanding, on the other hand, or to fail to make realistic decisions, is to contribute to the irrationality with which other men must then grapple; it is to throw new irrational factors into their environment. It is also to subtract oneself from the attraction of him who through honesty to our drive to realistic understanding invites us to participate in his light and his creative work. To work against understanding is to contribute to the burdens of other men. It is to fail to have been as creative as one might have been. And it is to have turned aside from God.

The evils of human life, then, are swelled by the irrational choices of men. The crimes of Hitler generate a misery, a bitterness, and a cynicism that affect millions of persons in one generation, and others in future generations as well. A father's careless treatment of his child may continue to echo in the lives of his grandchildren. A teacher's omissions or biases may color the minds of his students all their lives.

The world in which we live is, thus, a world of probability, risk, striving, and failure. That it is a reasonably good world is attested by all those who are content to confine their hopes within its horizons. Many nonbelievers appear to find it a good and an attractive world. Many give allegiance to intelligence, friendship, love, communication, art, beauty. They claim to do so despite man's impenetrable fate. But their very choice of values is, to those who believe in God, a confirmation of the power of intelligence and love in this world. Those who trust intelligence and love appear to exemplify what is good, noble, admirable in man. And in this way atheistic humanism becomes a motive for belief. For fidelity to understanding, friendship, creativity—the values carved out of nihilism—seem to believers to be the attraction exerted on men's hearts by him who is the source of man's drive to understand.

To say that God is good, therefore, is to say that he is the source of honesty, friendship, creativity—of those instincts and dispositions that follow upon fidelity to understanding. To say that there are evils in the world is to state a matter of fact. To say that God is omnipotent and could have prevented those evils if he wished is to state a truism. To say that God is not good, because he did not prevent the evil that happened to a relative, a friend, or oneself is to say more than the facts allow. For if God has drawn the suffering ones to himself, their fundamental good, is he evil? To cease believing in God because evils have happened is to have refused to move on to the true God, after having exposed a counterfeit. For to believe in the true God is not to anticipate a change in the probabilities of the historical order, such that one's own historical interests, needs, and desires are fulfilled. Man's good is not whatever he happens to commend, desire, approve, or need, but a life faithful to understanding. When aspirations which understanding recommends are in conflict, those most basic in the light of the drive to understand are to be preferred. "Though he will slay me, yet will I love him," Job confessed, bearing witness in the midst of evil to the basic meaning of good that applies, in different ways, both to God and to man.

3. The Two Mysteries

To say that God is good is not, moreover, to pretend foolishly to have penetrated into the two mysteries in which God's decisions lie hid. Granted a universe of emergent probabilities, a universe of waste, loss, and risk, the fact of evil is no surprise. If you want such a universe, including men such as we, you accept evils. But why God chose such a universe rather than another, except that in his eyes it is a good universe, no man can know; only the man pretending to be God would presume to judge. The reasons for God's choices are beyond legitimate inquiry, in our present state. For we can know that God exists, but not what he is like; we cannot read his mind, nor take a superior point of view.

But there is also a second mystery we cannot penetrate. If, in the world as it is, there is to be a military battle, we can anticipate that some men will die in it. We may even be able, with some accuracy, to predict the number who will die. But why this man should die, and not that other, we do not comprehend; the reasons for the destinies of individuals escape our penetration. The good are not always rewarded; the evil often prosper. Life is not a morality play. The judgment of God does not regularly assist those faithful to understanding with peace, prosperity, lack of suffering. On the contrary, they sometimes suffer more severely than those who turn away from creativity, love, and intelligence. Belief in God is not normally rewarded by events; sun and rain are indiscriminate. Even inwardly, the nonbeliever may feel contentment, while the believer may experience emptiness. God is truly a hidden God; there appears to be no earthly way of penetrating his singular designs, except by remaining faithful to one's understanding, doing what one must—and waiting.

Quite properly then, we understand that we cannot understand why this world is as it is, nor why this individual, family, or group should suffer, while other individuals, families, groups, do not. These two mysteries arising from the fact of evil are simply impenetrable. By fidelity to understanding and to love, however, we can affirm the value of these signs of God's presence among us; for such fidelity and love seem to be our best anticipations of what he himself is like. Nevertheless, the fact of evil often tempts believers to believe that their hunger to understand is in vain, that their anticipation of a transcendent intelligent subject is an illusion. For the fact of evil is an apparent defeat for understanding and hence for God. Why does he tolerate such defeats? At times, we wish that God were more straightforward. We cry out in desperation: "Say something clearly. Speak!" There never is an answer.

John Stuart Mill once conceived a simpler design for the world than the one we observe at present:

If the creator of mankind willed that men should all be virtuous, his designs are as completely baffled as if he had willed that they should all be happy. . . . If the law of all creatures were justice and the creator omnipotent, then in whatever amount suffering and happiness might be dispensed to the world, each person's share of them would be exactly proportioned to that person's good or evil deeds; no human being would have a worse lot than another, without worse deserts; accident or favouritism would have no part in such a world, but every human life would be the playing out of a drama constructed like a perfect moral tale.[19]

It is only with some pain that even philosophers relinquish such Sunday School designs in order to embrace the intricacies of our real destiny.

In the face of the real world, then, we retain our freedom. Our problem is whether to disbelieve in God because of the fact of evil, or to believe in him in spite of it. The irony is that in either case one must, if one is to justify one's life, remain faithful to understanding, friendship, creativity. One must be resigned to those tragedies one cannot prevent. One must labor for a reasonably just, prosperous, peaceful community of men on earth. One must discriminate between tyranny and freedom, between unjust and just social orders. The believer is sometimes tempted to despair. The nonbeliever is sometimes tempted to hope. Meanwhile, God does not speak, save through that necessity by which men justify whatever choice they make. For why, in a radically unintelligible world, would there be this drive to justify oneself? What does this drive signify?

There is also, however, the question raised by Professor Aiken in the essay with which we began this chapter: "If [God] has no hand in the evil, how then could He be said consistently to have a hand in the good? When we commit murder, the sin is ours. But, then, when we are loving, kind, or just, must not the credit and the praise be ours as well?"[20] God is the source of our drive to understand. Still, to turn away from this drive is a prerogative of our freedom, even though it be an uncritical yielding to our own interest, needs, and biases. Such an unintelligent or ill-willed choice is entirely due to our initiative. On the other hand, to remain faithful to our drive to understand is to remain faithful to its source. Thus, the light by which we are loving, kind, or just is more God's than ours. It is good and praiseworthy of us to be faithful to this light. Without it, moreover, we would be unable to move beyond an uncritical yielding to our interests, needs, desires and biases. By our drive to understand, then, we are not wooden instruments in the hands of God. We are autonomous and capable of evil. But we are indebted to him for our very autonomy: for the source of inquiry and freedom by which we define our identity and choose our destiny.[21] The good we do is done in his light; the evil, apart from it.

We need not go down on all fours in order to praise God. We thank him by standing erect, by exercising our freedom, by being faithful to our drive to understand—by becoming what we are capable of. We praise him by walking against the winds that blow in the darkness, despite the irrationalities and evils which dwell within us and lie in wait for us. We honor him by our pragmatism and our common sense. We are humble before him by our grasp of the plain fact—difficult to keep in mind—that each of us is a not especially central item in a universe of enormous spatial and temporal dimensions.

The critical religious mind does not relish mystery, though it recognizes heights and depths it cannot penetrate. It concentrates on walking step by step in the slender but ever-present light of conscience. It understands that a love for objective and searing honesty, which is usually embarrassing and often shattering to self-esteem, is man's distant share in the life of God. When the human spirit shares that love it participates from afar in the communication of God's proper life. And when we fail so to love, the fault appears to lie not in our stars but in ourselves.

7 ❖

AN EFFECTIVE HUMANISM

1. God Against Man

The most common argument against belief today, however, is not that belief in God is impossible because of theoretical difficulties; the theoretical difficulties appear merely to furnish an excuse. The most pressing difficulties of belief in God seem to lie in the historical order, in the behavior, ideas, and programs of believers.[1] Christianity was for a period the religion of Western culture; by the time the civilization of that period decayed and its deficiencies became apparent, Christianity was so identified with the past that it seemed unable to survive the breakthrough of the West toward a new form of civilization. Bishops who live in princely palaces; religious metaphors borrowed from an agricultural society; a church authority whose conceptions of obedience and freedom are feudal or baroque; an ethic shaped by and shaping the interests of the middle classes—these remain today as the residue of the past. Contemporary forms of religious faith require a man to live a double life: to think once in the modes of the past, and again in the modes of contemporary life. In the interests of economy and fidelity to oneself, it seems simpler not to believe. One could live as nobly, and far more effectively.

The classical protest of the man of unbelief is that belief divides his conscience, by pitting the sacred against the profane.

Meanwhile, he notes, religious persons indulge in the secular fashions of a bygone age. It is impossible for a religious man not to be *both* secular *and* religious; he must live on earth. Why divide what is single? Organized religion appears merely to be hypocritical in denouncing the secularism of the present time in favor of the secularism of the past.

To become a whole man, it sometimes seems, one must cease to believe. For many of those who belong to an organized religion waste more than half their energies bringing their organization to *aggiornamento*, arguing merely for room to work and breathe, and another quarter of their energy assuring nonbelievers that they don't "have a hidden premise up their sleeve." So little actual work gets done in living as one ought, and in helping to diminish the amount of suffering in the world, that despair and fatigue begin to choke out belief.

Ludwig Feuerbach put the dilemma in classic form in his Heidelberg lectures of 1848. His aim, he boldly announced, was to convert "the friends of God into the friends of man, believers into thinkers, worshippers into workers, candidates for the other world into students of this world, Christians, who are on their own confession half-animal and half-angel, into men—whole men."[2] Religion in the West has often been described as a tug-of-war between God and man, as if the two were antagonists. Feuerbach drew the conclusion: "To enrich God, man must become poor; that God may be all, man must be nothing."[3]

The reasons for atheism, however, are not one but many. A fallacious extolling of God's transcendence, for example, at the expense of man's own limited but necessary responsibilities to himself and his world, has often made a caricature of religion. If religion is a private affair between an individual and his transcendent God, religion is irrelevant to social, political, and cultural life. Moreover, it seems to distort a man's honesty, even to himself. The objections that can be lodged against religion on this ground are many:

1. In a choice between fidelity to self and fidelity to God, a believer must be faithful to God. But what, then, has he to offer God but the empty husk of his humanity?

2. To serve God is to lose one's autonomy, and to be vulnerable to the illusions that grow thick and fast where critical intelligence is relinquished.

3. To believe in God is to abdicate science and common sense. Belief in God is like belief in Santa Claus, or belief that suicide for the Emperor is a religious act—a myth which good sense does not support.

4. Belief in God is, for some, the exigence of an incurable cosmic optimism; and for others, the exigence of an obsession with guilt and the need for justification.

5. Attention given to God is attention taken from man. Religious belief blocks effective and needed social reform. Religious resignation dampens the fervor of cultural renewal. Where religion thrives today, nations are backward and tyrannies of all sorts are accepted. Where atheism abounds, an impulse is given the sciences, the arts, and social reconstruction.

These objections operate on two levels. At times, they are to be taken as theoretical objections: religion must *always* lead to such or such a conclusion. At other times, they are to be taken as historical observations: religion has *so far* in history led to such or such a conclusion. Both these levels seem operative, for example, in the complaint of Sidney Hook: "No matter how religion is reconstructed, there will always be a difference between the approach of a secular, rational, and ethical humanism to the problems of man and society and the approach of religion. History cannot be disregarded so lightly. The language of religion carries with it a mood of acceptance and resignation to the world as we find it, which tends to dissipate the mood of social change and reform."[4]

The principle of social change and reform, however, is not a "mood." Change and reform, if they are to be justified before the bar of responsible opinion, derive from the light of the drive to understand as it is made to focus on the limitations of an historical system. The principle of social change has, therefore, the same root as the principle of religion: both are based in the drive to understand. If, historically, religion has often been identified as a conservative force in society, a new religion has often worked also as a revolutionary force. Moreover, the prophetic tradition, even in long-established religions, still furnishes the rhetoric and thought-patterns of messianic, atheistic social revolutions.

But one can cite "history" on either side of this, as of almost any, question. What is at stake for us today is whether Christianity and Judaism, and indeed Islam, Buddhism, and other world religions, can become secularized in the new technological and world culture, as they once were secularized in earlier cultures. What is at stake is whether belief in God needs to "dissipate" the energies of the drive to understand, as it inquires into and criticizes the present social order; or whether belief in God itself can inspire the social reforms required for the coming civilization. This point is proved by deeds, not by pledges. The document on "The Church in the Modern World" proposed at the Second Vatican Council is a step in the right direction. But much more important than what believers say is, What do believers *do*?

On the other hand, there is another line of argument in Professor Hook's view. It is surely not required that everyone accept Professor Hook's version of what constitutes a realistic reform of the social order, or anyone else's view. We have had occasion to notice earlier[5] that Mr. Hook is something of an instrumentalist; he does not linger over-much on the demands of first awarenesss, insight, reflection, or the drive to understand, except insofar as their exercise yields matters of prediction and control in the practical order. By contrast, Professor Reinhold Niebuhr seems to express a more fully naturalistic view; Professor Hook's naturalism appears to be based on an abstraction.

Professor Niebuhr has written, for example, of his own "increasing appreciation of the organic factors in social life in contrast to the tendencies stemming from the Enlightenment which blind modern men to the significance of these organic factors, and treat the human community and its instruments of order and justice as if they were purely artifacts." He adds: "I believe that, ultimately considered, this is a religious issue."[6]

Religion is based on the drive to understand: that is why the difference between the organic and the atomistic view is ultimately a religious issue. The rationalistic programs of the Enlightenment, based upon common sense and science, commonly neglect the data of intelligent subjectivity. As a consequence, they take both the human individual and human society as less than they are; both individuals and society are enlisted in the service of an abstraction, a "good life" in which each man plays a "useful" role as part of an ongoing machine. Such programs conceive of man technologically, and subject him to contrivances and experiments; they take him as an object. But man is more than an object. When all the goods of health, education, security, and wealth are distributed to him, he still hungers to know who he is; he feels the invitation of the greatest good, who addresses him from afar, through his drive to understand.

Furthermore, as Niebuhr writes, "Any conservatism which is merely interested in the preservation of some *status quo* would be anathema for anyone who had drawn inspiration from the Old Testament prophets."[7] Religion based on the drive to understand has no need to "take the world as it finds it." On the contrary, the command in Genesis was "Increase and multiply and possess the earth." A religious man is entitled to take refuge in resignation only when he has done all that is in him and can do no more. Moreover, since man is not omnipotent, both believer and nonbeliever are obliged to learn resignation; neither is privileged beyond the other. Their unlimited drive to understand, however, preserves in both the springs of hope and vision.

A religion based on the drive to understand, finally, takes

cognizance of the objections raised against historical religion. Men of belief are permitted to learn from the mistakes, failings, and temporally conditioned horizons of the past; and to move on to further horizons. Religion based on fidelity to the drive to understand can be a most effective instrument of social and political reform.[8] It can also serve as a bridge of unity among men of various religious traditions. For the vocabulary, conceptions, theological systems, and liturgies of the various religious traditions are specifications of one same unlimited drive to understand. God is truly named by reference to the unlimited drive to understand, despite the importance of such historically conditioned contexts. Men do not have to share in the same religious tradition in order to share belief in the one same God. However important the distinctions dear to each tradition, the radical hunger of man's intelligence is a bond of religious unity whose appeal is transcultural.[9]

The point remains that the proof of religion's effectiveness in renewing, deepening, and reforming human life lies not in proposals but in actions. If religion is merely a relic of the secular myths of a prescientific era, religion will thrive wherever science has not penetrated, but as science advances it will move increasingly to the periphery of human life. If it is based on the drive to understand, and is inextricably linked to man's identity as man, it will help to humanize a scientific era. Professor Hook himself has seen this possibility. He has on at least one occasion seen something good in Professor Tillich's "being-itself," a phrase that seems to be the ontological equivalent of our cognitional way of naming God. Professor Hook writes:

I must confess that at certain moments I find Tillich's approach to religion attractive as a kind of moral strategy. For if God is not an entity or a being but being-itself, no religion truly oriented to Him or It could be persecutory. All religions would be equal in their sense of stuttering inadequacy as they sought to articulate that which was beyond articulation. Full of humility and awe before the Power of Being, they would revise or reinterpret their religious symbols in order to express the highest moral reaches of human experience. They would seek more explicitly than in the past to devise symbols which would integrate rather than disintegrate human personality. They would turn to the findings of modern psychology, sociology, and moral theory for leads and material rather than go adventuring on an impossible quest for being. They would provide aesthetic and emotional support for the various types of humanisms and ethical culture whose rituals are so often dreary and funereal. Religion would forever cease its warfare against science and remove its "no trespass" signs from the roads of intellectual inquiry into the mysteries of mind and spirit.[10]

A religion based on the drive to understand does not pit God against man. To worship God is as natural for man as to develop and to employ scientific method. "Naturalism" is an abstraction, a failure of nerve concerning the dynamism of the drive to understand. It appears to be, moreover, an historical and visceral reaction against certain forms of religious life, certain conceptions of religious reality, and certain influences of religious institutions on the social and political order. To be enlightened has come to mean to be enlightened from religion. To be intelligent has come to mean to deny that the dynamism of one's intelligence has its source in an intelligent subject, who is also the source of the intelligibility, such as it is, of the real. Such an inversion is truly curious. A systematic study of the psychology of unbelief has yet to be completed; it has been much more fashionable, until recently, to psychoanalyze the believer.[11]

For a religion based on the drive to understand does not, in fact, compromise one's honesty; on the contrary, it depends upon it. It insists that fidelity to God is through, and only through, fidelity to one's self; one cannot please God by acting contrary to one's reflective, open conscience. Such religion does not require a surrender of critical intelligence; its only defense against false gods is through the exercise of critical intelligence. It does not require the abdication of science and common sense, although it has its origin and justification neither in science nor in common sense. Its origin and justification lie in reflection upon one's own intelligent subjectivity, which is prior to science and to common sense, and is the source of their origin and justification. It does not require cosmic optimism, nor does it spring from an obsession with guilt. Rooted in critical intelligence, it seeks only what is true about the cosmos, entertaining neither sentimental illusions nor unwarranted feelings of guilt. Nevertheless, just because it is so deeply and purely based, it accuses the self of countless and inevitable infidelities to its own light. No perceptive man pretends to be without illusions which feed his ego, and tend to make his judgments pivot not on what is real but on what he would like the real to be. But if such accusations of the self against the self are true, so the guilt feelings arising from them are not obsessive but realistic; and the hope of living perfectly faithful to understanding becomes the measure of our frailty.

Belief in God based on fidelity to understanding is based upon fidelity to oneself. In discovering one's own identity, one discovers God. The policy of life by which one chooses to be faithful to understanding leads, at one and the same time, to one's own identity and to God. To seek one is to seek the other. Man, if our view of religion is correct, is naturally religious.

2. Corruption and Community

Finally, one of the greatest obstacles to belief in God is the complacency of believers. It is not the adulterers, the takers of bribes, the licentious, whose conduct induces disbelief. It is the righteous, the solid citizens, the people of good reputation in the community. Such believers show few signs of ever having encountered the terrifying God; nor do they appear to live in that cold night of belief in which he is most truly found. Their god seems to be an idol, the idol of habit, routine, sentiment, and self-congratulation. By their words and actions, they treat God as a vague guarantor of the good order which makes them secure. He is the projection of that superego which keeps them conscientious when no one is looking. In his name, they dare to preach mere law and order, rather than also the freedom and inquiry through which the living God is found. Their god is the dead god of the middle classes.

For many a sensitive American Catholic—not to speak of Protestants and Jews—belief in God sometimes becomes intolerable. It would not be an exaggeration to say that the greatest source of unbelief among believers is the Church itself. To be honest on this point is to use harsh words, words which in any case are frequent in private conversation. Many hundreds of thousands of believers sometimes ask: "How can this preposterous Church be divine?" The families of many of those who seek God go through the forms of their religion, and take the truth of religion for granted; religion is a habit, like an old pair of slippers. Where is God? countless young people have asked—at least in the days before liturgical reform—Where is God in the impersonal, machinelike rendering of the Mass, in the vulgar and narrow-minded sermon in which the Gospels are not preached, in (as it seems to very many) the automated receiving of regular communion? He seems obscured by a tissue of myths, fears, routines, and lethargy, together with a systematic deadening of the drive to understand: "Beware of intellectual pride, do not inquire, pray, be humble, do not lose your faith, apostasy is worse than never having been baptized."

Add to this the activism of the clergy: "When in doubt, build"—building, ever building, and collecting funds. Catholicism, one is often told in conversation, seems to be an efficient shell without spirit; its churches seem to be stone boxes more like supermarts than homes of the human spirit; its moral code seems more Jansenist than evangelical. American Catholicism, Gabriel

Marcel once remarked, seems to act like a sect jealous of its own interests, reputation, and cohesiveness.

A high proportion of its bishops, the faithful complain, seem characteristically timid, prudent, cautious men whose great ideal is not to step out of line, not to offend ecclesiastical proprieties, not to cause trouble, not to be tempted by a new idea. The clean-shaven *monsignori* who run the chancery, the school systems, the seminaries, and the largest parishes, seem to be businessmen, golfers, connoisseurs of restaurants, well trained to the books of canon law, in love with the Church as an institution, money raisers, enemies of "secularism," proud of the Church as a bulwark against atheistic communism, good company for brother priests and for congenial parishioners, sometimes prayerful, and faithful eunuchs for "the kingdom of God." Is this the community of believers of which the Gospels speak? Have the blood and suffering of the ages come to this?

But if some of the clergy are easy symbols of the transformation of Christianity from a way of life to a mere efficient institution, others are the source of whatever hope remains. The younger clergy are full of promise, whereas large numbers of the laity appear to have long ago been poisoned by the invisible, odorless gas of apathy. The problem no longer is lay versus clerical. The problem now is life of the spirit versus death. Many priests, as well as many laymen, are suffering in a night of faith; they find it difficult to believe that God is alive in the people who continue to fill the churches. Many priests and sisters are empty of consolation.

I speak frankly: one looks around, listens, and observes; and one asks: "Can there be a God, and do we know him?" Many can no longer describe without violent emotion the falsehood, complacency, absence of the spirit of inquiry, and the distorted moral sense of our poorly led religious people, who in the main do not desire better leaders. Perhaps it has been too large a jump from the farms and sheds of Europe to the executive offices, real estate firms, doctors', lawyers', and mayors' offices, mills, and factories of America, in three generations. The inquiring drive of the human spirit, at any rate, seems almost smothered by the competition, aggressiveness, complacency, and smugness of American life.

Believers, clergy and lay, seem in the main and from the outside to be more pragmatic than the pragmatists would have them, more self-centered than the utilitarians depend upon, more conformist than the relativist requires, more secular than the secular idealist. They love their families. A kind of national kindliness, and friendliness, and informality, still thrive in many places. There are, no doubt, many unknown and hidden persons who eat the daily bread of naked faith, who have suffered much, and still trust the living God. But the vast, efficient weight of organized religion hangs on the shoulders of sensitive Catholics who try to maintain the belief of their fathers, and burdens them with sadness.

Yet the citizen does not flee the United States because its political life is choked by mediocrity, compromise, and venality. One does not abandon democracy because few people vote and fewer still exercise the vigilance upon which good government depends. One does not give up faith in freedom because vast numbers of men shun its responsibilities. Religion too is not a private but a social phenomenon; not one man alone, but all, share the drive to understand which is its root. History is heavy with failures and unrealized possibilities; what men do is ever a distant shadow of what they might do, could they be wholly faithful to themselves. Neither in politics nor in religion does a realist expect more than a tincture of virtue, the tiniest spark of pure and naked belief. And thus one retains a membership one cannot, in any case, improve upon. It has been said from the beginning: "Lord, to whom shall we go?"

The natural alliance in American society, however, is between the men of critical reflection, believing and nonbelieving; and their mutual enemy is the huckster, who competes with them for the soul of the American people.[12] There is a serious danger that the huckster will win in this struggle, and choke religion and intelligence to death. For the American intellectual has come to be as disdainful of the culture of the ordinary man as the ordinary man is distrustful of the egghead.

Yet ordinary people and intellectuals need each other.[13] A man who loses his roots in the people, Dostoevsky said, soon becomes an atheist. In America, it is true, the tide of philosophy and the social sciences runs against belief in God, and intelligent believers are reduced to silence, while the religion of the people is vulgarized by the hucksters; there seems no escape but in atheism. Yet the root of religion does not lie in the inarticulate tradition of the people; it appears to lie there only because the advance of modern science has drawn our attention away from the depths of intelligent subjectivity. We speak easily, now, about the needs and inquiries of pragmatic extroversion, about prediction and control, about the solving of problems. We do not yet speak well about the deep, unstructured, unlimited claims of the drive to understand. We know better what we are needed for than who we are; of what "use" a man is in the march of progress, and what "contribution" he can make, than what his personal destiny may be.

The malaise that grips us is that we are subjects who seem to know that we have a unique identity, but cannot articulate it. Each of us is daily called upon to lead a "creative" life and to sacrifice himself for society. Is this so very different from being called upon to love our neighbor as ourselves, and to love God through loving those in need?

Unbelief seems to ask of us no more than belief does: the same nakedness before a hidden God; the same pursuit of understanding, friendship, creativity; the same risks in one same world of emergent probabilities, surds, and evils; the same lack of consolation, voices in the heart, or assurances; the same moral and intellectual responsibilities. The authentic believer and the authentic nonbeliever share a very similar interior development. Both seek to be faithful to the drive to understand.

What difference is there, then, between a man who refuses to name God or to "believe" in him, even though he is scrupulously faithful to understanding, cherishes friendships, values creativity—and a man who through the same fidelity, experience of friendship, and hunger to create does give a name to God and does believe that he exists? Both men live a life similar in nearly every respect. Secular saint and religious saint alike strive to diminish the amount of suffering in the world; neither one sees God. One says Yes to understanding, love, creativity, but No to God. The other thinks that the first Yes implies the second.

It is easy to see how some men will choose one of these ways, and others the other. In the present darkness which is our life on earth, it is of basic importance that as many men as possible say the first Yes. Since, in any case, God remains hidden and inconceivable, perhaps the illation to the second Yes, made in words, is not required. Many of those who do not make that illation are no doubt more dear to God, and of his mind, than those who have his name frequently upon their lips.

In the service of the hidden God, there is a band of hidden servants, inside and outside the ranks of organized religion. For organized religion is the outer social form, the institutional structure, the requirement of man's flesh and blood. Not all whose names are written on its rolls appear to believe in the living God. Not all who serve that God are on its rolls. Better to belong to the hidden brotherhood, better to serve the living God, than merely to go through the outer forms. Nevertheless, agnosticism is not an acceptable alternative to one who has already known the Church; so long as there are men of flesh and blood, historical men, there will have to be slow, blundering, imperfect religious institutions; and it is, ironically, largely through their offices that the prophetic spirit exposing their inadequacy is kept alive. The purpose of religious institutions is not to glorify themselves, but to criticize themselves, and to denounce the idols they constantly erect in the place of the living and the hidden God.

It is because the churches of the West became inhabited with idols that the sharp nose of Nietzsche detected the odor of God's death. It is the dishonesties of believers, and the stupid idols they worship, which make unbelief not only plausible but even compelling among those faithful to understanding in our generation. And it is rather in the ranks of such faithful ones, inside or outside the churches, that an honest man would wish to stand, than among the placid faces of the virtuous.

EPILOGUE

The question we have been facing is how belief differs from unbelief and whether there is evidence which favors one side or the other. We may summarize our present findings. Belief is opposed to unbelief as one radical interpretation of human destiny to another. By belief in God, a man accepts the universe as radically personal; he believes that a Person who is the intelligent source of the world draws men, through whatever evils, to himself. By nonbelief, a man interprets the universe by an image of impersonality: of chance, of functionalism, of the laws of physics, of the absurd.

The choice of belief springs from confidence in the centrality of the phenomena of awareness, the drive to understand, insight, and critical reflection in this universe. The choice of nonbelief springs from discounting these phenomena in favor of others: laws of physics more basic than those of psychology; the evils of existence; the hiddenness of the Person believers trust. Believers believe that the human person, though infinitesimal and seemingly insignificant among the galaxies, is the interpretive key to the universe and to the presence and activity of God. Nonbelievers value the human person as much as believers in the conduct of their lives. But they refuse to leap from that lived value to a belief that the human person is an image, however weak, of an infinite God, the source of the universe and the friend of man.

The evidence by which it seems possible to decide between

these views is different from all other evidence. No empirical test of the usual kind is possible. What is required is reflection upon the drive which leads us to demand an empirical test. The believer notes that the human person cannot, realistically and worthily, be treated by another person as a thing; and that the drive to understand which has driven men to whatever achievements of understanding they have attained is conspicuously successful in dealing with the real. The real seems to be heuristically intelligible—intelligible in principle, worthy of inquiry. It seems plausible to suppose that it has an intelligent source. This supposition is strengthened by the experience of living according to it. If one believes in a personal God, light is shed upon the unparalleled respect one is inclined to pay to other persons, as persons, and upon the intelligibility of the policy of being faithful to understanding, friendship, and creativity.

On the supposition of nonbelief, there is no personal God. The nonbeliever may, as well as any believer, maintain in his conduct the policy of being faithful to understanding, friendship, and creativity. But such a policy seems to be an isolated measure, for mutual defense and comfort, in an impersonal universe. The acceptance of nonbelief makes the human person finally insignificant, personally and collectively. The human person is not seen as an interpretive key to the universe.

Nevertheless, although the human person is humble and puny, he does seem to be the source of science and morality, and indeed of the whole project of interpretation. As the source of this project, he also seems to be its key. He interprets; and he is the key to what he interprets.

The logic of the decision between belief and unbelief is a peculiar logic. For it involves reflection not so much on premises and conclusions as on the drive in us which is the generator of premises and conclusions. The ultimate question is whether this drive is in vain—whether it tells the tale of an idiot, signifying nothing—or whether it signifies that a God of intelligence and love makes known his presence through that drive, calling man to be faithful to understanding and to love. Is intelligent subjectivity merely a function of world process, or that and also a testimony of God's presence?

The key to belief or unbelief hinges upon our interpretation of our own drive to understand. The decision is rooted in self-knowledge, and by it we respond to what we take ourselves to be and define what we shall become. They are wise who do not make a mistake in defining their own identity. They are foolish who try to live while avoiding a decision, for to *live* one way rather than another is already to have *decided*. Agnosticism is impossible as a policy of life.

Because a man sometimes understands and tries to be faithful to understanding and to love, he understands and defines his identity as a person in a more than functional way. Because of his understanding of himself as a person, he concludes that there is a God; otherwise, he is unintelligible to himself. He sometimes speaks with him, sight unseen, voice unheard, hidden in the night; and speaks not alone but with many other men.

It seems to me that the nonbeliever is mistaken in his interpretation of human experience. But I admit that he may be correct. The serious nonbeliever and the serious believer, moreover, share a hidden unity of spirit. When both do all they can to be faithful to their understanding and to love, and to the immediate task of diminishing the amount of suffering in the world, the intention of their lives is similar, even though their conceptions of what they are doing are different. Such a unity in the intention of two lives seems in the end to be more profound than a unity on the conceptual level. Some Christians, moreover, feel closer to nonbelievers like Albert Camus than to other Christians whom they know, in their understanding of the fundamental dynamism of the human spirit.

It appears to be this unity in intentionality that leads believers to "baptize" nonbelievers, and nonbelievers to say that believers are, underneath it all, nonbelievers. Belief and nonbelief are rival conceptualizations of human intentionality. It seems, however, more important that believer and nonbeliever should *practice* the same fidelity to understanding and to love, the same hope which leads to creativity and the same resignation which results from grappling with the real, than that they should *conceive of* these, or of their further significance, in the same way.

Believer and nonbeliever are, each of them, human persons. It is more important for them to live as such than to share the same theories about what it means to be a human person on this earth. To decide between belief or unbelief is of the utmost importance, for such a decision radically alters one's conception of oneself. But for those who even before such a decision are living according to fidelity to understanding, the intention and dynamism of their life do not change. They have merely "found themselves."

Toward that goal, believer and nonbeliever are both voyagers. In the darkness in which the secret courses of human lives lie hidden, men are sometimes closer together, sometimes farther apart, than appearances indicate. For this reason, many men look searchingly into the eyes of others, seeking a brother, a sister, who could be anywhere. Among us thrives a brotherhood of inquiry and concern, even of those who disagree in interpreting the meaning of inquiry—the meaning of human spirit—in the darkness in which we live.

NOTES

FOREWORD

1. George Braziller: New York, 1964, p. 253.
2. *Ibid.*, pp. 253-55.

INTRODUCTION: A Dialectical Inquiry

1. *The Fall*, Alfred A. Knopf: New York, 1961, p. 133.
2. It is a curious fact that many men of affairs, like Dag Hammarskjöld in *Markings* (Alfred A. Knopf: New York, 1964), seem quietly to maintain a deep and pure faith in God, often apart from the churches; and many professors on the campuses seem to do the same. Nevertheless, large numbers of philosophers, psychologists, and social scientists seem to be quite certain that such faith is unintelligent and mythical. Those who take one range of views regarding science and verifiability, and superimpose them on the stuff of human experience, seem most inclined to fall in the latter class. Those who accept some human experiences that they cannot successfully articulate in words and scientific concepts seem inclined to rest in a faith which is virtually silent in the company of the "men of clear light." At the present moment, the articulation of nonbelief seems an easier task, since by academic convention a certain view of verifiability is accepted despite difficulties in justifying it.
3. If I say very little about love in this book, it is because of a conviction that genuine love is guided by realistic understanding; and that love which is unrealistic is ultimately destructive, both of lover and beloved. But I also take realistic understanding to be incomplete until a man is joined in conversation, in presence, in communion, with others who share that understanding, respond to its drive and direction, and invite its response to theirs. In general, Eric Fromm's classic, *The Art of Loving* (Harper & Row: New York, 1956), expresses such

an outlook. See also Frederick E. Crowe, "Complacency and Concern in the Thought of St. Thomas," *Theological Studies*, 20 (1959), 1-39, 198-230, 343-95.

4. Sartre, *op. cit.*, pp. 110-11, 253.

5. ". . . when suddenly God saw me. I felt His gaze inside my head and on my hands. I whirled about in the bathroom, horribly visible, a living target. Indignation saved me. I flew into a rage against so crude an indiscretion . . . He never looked at me again." *Ibid.*, p. 102.

Sartre adds: "Failing to take root in my heart, He vegetated in me for awhile, then He died. Whenever anyone speaks to me about Him today, I say, with the easy amusement of an old beau who meets a former belle: 'Fifty years ago, had it not been for that misunderstanding, that mistake, the accident that separated us, there might have been something between us.'" *Ibid.*, pp. 102-3.

6. *Ibid.*, pp. 253-54.

7. University of Chicago Press: Chicago, 1958.

8. Longman's, Green and Co.: London, 1957.

9. See Albert Camus, *The Myth of Sisyphus*, Random House (Vintage Book): New York, 1960, p. 38.

10. *I and Thou* (2nd ed.), Charles Scribner's Sons: New York, 1958.

11. Gabriel Marcel, *The Mystery of Being*, 2 vols., Gifford Lectures, Henry Regnery: Chicago, 1960.

12. "Birth, Suicide, and the Doctrine of Creation: an Exploration of Analogies," *Mind* 68 (1959), pp. 309-21.

13. *Religious Language*, The Macmillan Company: New York, 1963.

14. *Thought and Action*, The Viking Press: New York, 1960.

15. Cf. T. S. Eliot, "Tradition and the Individual Talent," *The Selected Essays of T. S. Eliot*, Harcourt, Brace & World: New York, 1950; and B. F. Skinner, *Science and Human Behavior*, The Macmillan Company: New York, 1953.

16. In *Wisdom and Love in St. Thomas Aquinas* (Marquette University Press: Milwaukee, Wisconsin, 1951), Etienne Gilson touches on the traditional place of self-knowledge in Greek and medieval philosophy (pp. 1-4, 25-29), the role of will and personality in speculative inquiry (pp. 13-18, 30-33), and the ability of one developed spirit to recognize another (pp. 7-8). The categories of M. Gilson in this brief study appear, however, to be somewhat rationalistic for the point he is making.

17. Mr. Wallace I. Matson, in *The Existence of God* (Cornell

University Press: Ithaca, N.Y., 1965), appears to have succumbed to this temptation. By "traditional," he appears to mean Kantian. He writes of mystics without offering evidence that he has read their testimony; he certainly does not grapple with it. He writes of God as though God were an object to be discovered by sensory or extrasensory perception, or else by some technique of deduction. Professor John Hicks describes Mr. Matson's study as a "slightly archaic exercise" (*The Saturday Review* 48 (1965), no. 6 (Feb. 6), p. 40). Mr. Matson understands "reason" in an odd way; he appears to overlook the many and subtle roles of intelligence in the establishment of criteria of inquiry and evidence, in the choice of a policy of life, in political and practical decisions, in the comparison and weighing of evidence, in one's sense of self-identity, and in criticizing, directing, and preserving one's loves. It is no wonder that he writes his inquiry as though he were wandering upon a strange, lunar landscape. Where he is searching, hardly anything living grows.

18. In *Pensées*, "Fragment 77," E. P. Dutton & Co. (paperback): New York, 1958, p. 13.

19. Thomas Aquinas, *Summa Theologica*, I, q. 4, a. 1, ad. 1, citing Gregory.

20. Lonergan, *op. cit.*, pp. 669-86.

ONE: THE CULTURAL CONTEXT

1. Cf. Martin E. Marty, *The Varieties of Unbelief*, Holt, Rinehart, & Winston: New York, 1964.

2. Cf. John Courtney Murray, S.J., *The Problem of God*, Yale University Press: New Haven, Conn., 1964.

3. "We have travelled far since Voltaire's day. . . . We have witnessed a failure of rational nerve; we have watched the prestige of reason decline. . . . Writers who were skeptical and uncompromising intellectuals only twenty years ago are taking refuge in old religions of the West and even older Eastern mysteries. The fugitives from reason are following many paths, but their numbers are impressive. . . . Whether or not this flight is a major movement in the intellectual history of man, whether or not the rational tide, after its long run, is destined to be borne backward by a rising tide of faith, remains to be demonstrated." Ben Ray Redman, Editor's Introduction, *The Portable Voltaire*, The Viking Press: New York, 1960, pp. 45-46.

Professor Paul Edwards of New York University has collected Bertrand Russell's essays against religion because the tide of religious propaganda has recently risen so high that "a re-statement of the unbeliever's case seems particularly desirable." He thinks the question of belief and unbelief is biased in favor of belief. "Outside the classrooms of the better colleges the negative side to this question is hardly ever presented." See Editor's Introduction, Bertrand Russell, *Why I Am Not a Christian*, Simon and Schuster (paperback): New York, 1957, p. xii.

4. Cf. Emmanuel Cardinal Suhard, *The Church Today: Growth or Decline?*, Fides Press: Notre Dame, Ind., 1948.

5. Random House (Vintage Book): New York, 1956, p. 305.

6. Cf. Harry R. Davis and Robert C. Good, eds., *Reinhold Niebuhr on Politics*, Charles Scribner's Sons: New York, 1960, pp. 12-25.

7. On the trickiness of cultural unanimity, see Lonergan's two chapters on "Common Sense as Object" and "Common Sense as Subject," *op. cit.*

8. See "The Story of Theseus" in Plutarch's *Lives*, Modern Library Edition: New York, 1932, p. 14.

9. See John A. T. Robinson, *Honest to God*, The Westminster Press: Philadelphia, 1963. The quotation is from a review of this book by Thomas Merton, in *The Commonweal*, LXXX, 19 (August 21, 1964), p. 573.

10. Merton, *ibid.*

11. *Ibid.*, p. 576.

12. *Tractatus Logico-Philosophicus*, 6.52, Routledge & Kegan Paul: London, 1960.

13. *Ludwig Wittgenstein*, Oxford University Press: Oxford, 1959, p. 72.

14. Merton, *op. cit.*, p. 574.

15. See *ibid.*, p. 576.

16. A revisionary metaphysics is concerned not to describe the actual structure of our thought about the world, but "to produce a better structure," according to P. F. Strawson, *Individuals*, Methuen & Co.: London, 1961, Introduction, pp. 9 ff. By "revisionary" in the present context, however, I seem to mean what Professor Strawson means by a "descriptive" method, but one of fuller scope and greater generality than that now generally practiced.

17. See John Wisdom, "Gods," in Anthony Flew (ed.), *Logic and Language*, 1st Series, Blackwell: London, 1951; and the comment on this parable in "Theology and Falsification," Part VI of *New Essays in Philosophical Theology*, edited by Flew and McIntyre, SCM Press: London, 1958.

18. Gabriel Marcel refers to this attention as "creative fidelity." See, e.g., his essay "On the Ontological Mystery" in *The Philosophy of Existentialism*, Citadel Press: New York, 1961; and also his book *Creative Fidelity*, Farrar, Straus & Company: New York, 1964.

19. Josef Pieper, *A Guide to the Philosophy of St. Thomas Aquinas*, Random House: New York, 1962; see also his *Belief and Faith*, Random House: New York, 1963.

20. M. D. Chenu, O.P., *Toward Understanding St. Thomas*, Henry Regnery: Chicago, 1964.

21. Peter Hoenen, *Reality and Judgment According to St. Thomas*, Henry Regnery: Chicago, 1952.

22. James Collins, *Three Paths in Philosophy*, Henry Regnery: Chicago, 1962. One could also mention, of course, Étienne Gilson and Jacques Maritain, and several increasingly important writers, such as Joseph de Finance.

23. See Eliot's Introduction to the edition of Pascal's *Pensées*, published in paperback by E. P. Dutton & Co. in 1958. This essay is also included in *The Selected Essays of T. S. Eliot*, Harcourt, Brace & World: New York, 1950.

24. This theme recurs in Niebuhr's writings. See, e.g., his contributions to volume II of the *Library of Living Theology*, edited by Kegley and Bretall, which is dedicated to his work, pp. 19 ff. See also his *The Self and the Dramas of History*, Charles Scribner's Sons: New York, 1955.

25. Niebuhr writes: "The rational capacity of surveying the world, of forming general concepts and analyzing the wonder of the world, is thus but one aspect of what Christianity knows as 'spirit.' The self knows the world, insofar as it knows the world, because it stands outside both itself and the world, which means that it cannot understand itself except as it is understood from beyond itself and the world.

"This essential homelessness of the human spirit is the ground of all religion; for the self which stands outside itself and the world cannot find the meaning of life in itself or the world. It cannot identify meaning with causality in nature; for its freedom is obviously something different from the necessary causal links of nature. Nor can it identify the principle of meaning with rationality, since it transcends its own rational processes, so that it may, for instance, ask the question whether there is a relevance between its rational forms and the recurrences and forms of nature. It is this capacity of freedom which finally prompts great cultures and philosophies to transcend rationalism and to seek for the meaning of life in an unconditioned ground of existence." *The Nature and Destiny of Man* vol. I, Charles Scribner's Sons (paperback): New York, 1964, p. 14.

26. See his "Intellectual Autobiography" in Kegley and Bretall (eds.), *op. cit.*, p. 17.

27. *Ibid.*, pp. 17-18, 450.

TWO: PHILOSOPHY AS SELF-KNOWLEDGE

1. See Stuart Hampshire, *Thought and Action*, The Viking Press: New York, 1960, pp. 90 ff.

2. John Courtney Murray, *The Problem of God*, p. 119. See also Martin D'Arcy, *No Absent God*, Harper & Row: New York, 1962.

3. Murray, *op. cit.*, p. 120.

4. *Ibid.*, p. 118.

5. Bernard Lonergan, "Metaphysics as Horizon," *Gregorianum*, 44 (1963), pp. 307-18, and reprinted in *The Current* (Harvard-Radcliffe Catholic Club), 5 (1964), pp. 6-23. See also my "Philosophy and Fiction," *The Christian Scholar* 47 (1964), pp. 100-10.

6. "But, as confession is good for the soul, I must admit that I do not very much relish the conclusions toward which these conclusions point. I would rather allot to philosophy a sublimer task than the detection of the sources in linguistic idioms of recurrent misconstructions and absurd theories. But that it is at least this I cannot feel any serious doubt." In "Systematically Misleading Expressions," *Essays in Logic and Language*, 1st Series, A. Flew (ed.), Blackwell: London, 1951, p. 36. Flew refers to this passage as expressing "insight"; and Professor Ryle himself says frequently that forms of words "exhibit" their content. See Flew's Introduction, pp. 5-7, and Ryle's article, *passim*.

7. Dover Publications: New York (n.d.), chap. 2. Cf. John Passmore, *A Hundred Years of Philosophy*, Duckworth: London, 1962, pp. 388-93.

8. Various philosophers approach this point from various points of view. Those who have been especially helpful to me in their stress upon the fact that self-knowledge, recognized or unrecognized, is the source of philosophy have been Gabriel Marcel—particularly in *The Mystery of Being*, Henry Regnery: Chicago, 1960; Ortega y Gasset, *What is Philosophy?*, W. W. Norton: New York, 1960; Jacques Maritain in *The Range of Reason*, Charles Scribner's Sons: New York, 1952; *Existence and the Existence* (Image book), Doubleday & Company: New York, 1957; *Approaches to God*, Harper & Row: New

York, 1954; and Reinhold Niebuhr, *The Self and the Dramas of History*, Charles Scribner's Sons: New York, 1955. On the other hand, I recognize the need for working out these issues in a more pragmatic and empirical framework. And my main debt, of course, is to Bernard Lonergan.

9. *Nichomachean Ethics*, 1095*b*, pp. 1-13.

10. The Macmillan Company: New York, 1960, pp. 12-13.

11. See my "The Idealism of B. F. Skinner," *The Current* (Harvard-Radcliffe Catholic Club), 5 (1964), pp. 45-46.

12. Skinner, *Science and Human Behavior*, The Macmillan Company: New York, 1960, p. 283.

13. *Ibid.*

14. *Ibid.*, p. 285.

15. *The Essence of Christianity*, Harper & Row (Torchbook): New York, 1957, quoted by Karl Barth in the introductory essay, pp. xiii-iv, without exact reference.

16. See Walter J. Ong, S.J., "A Dialectic of Aural and Objective Correlatives," *The Barbarian Within*, The Macmillan Company: New York, 1962, pp. 26-40; and Robert P. Scharlemann, *Thomas Aquinas and John Gerhard*, Yale University Press: New Haven, Conn., 1964, esp. pp. 11-12, 24 ff.

17. *The Quest for Being*, St. Martin's Press: New York, 1961, p. 214.

18. *Ibid.*, p. 217.

19. *Ibid.*, p. 218.

20. *Ibid.*, p. 216.

21. *Ibid.*, p. 194.

22. *Ibid.*, pp. 194-95.

23. *Ibid.*, p. 195.

24. *Ibid.*

25. *Ibid.*, p. 207.

26. *Ibid.*, p. 195.

27. *Ibid.*, p. 216.

28. *Ibid.*, p. 207.

29. *Ibid.*, p. 216.

30. *Ibid.*, p. 217.

31. *Ibid.*, p. 216.

32. "Like some of one's moral beliefs, one's basic philosophical commitments are not easily surrendered for pragmatic successes—even of the purest kind." Harvard University Press: Cambridge, Mass., 1959, pp. 280-81, 284 ff., 268-78.

33. *Ibid.*, p. 277.

34. Newman, *The Grammar of Assent*, Doubleday & Company (Image Book): New York, 1958.

35. White, *op. cit.*, p. 278. Some of the criteria for scientific conscience appear to be efficacy in communication and in prediction, elegance, conceptual economy or simplicity, and a certain familiarity. See Nelson Goodman, *Fact, Fiction, and Forecast*, Harvard University Press: Cambridge, Mass., 1955, p. 38; and W. V. Quine, *From a Logical Point of View*, Harvard University Press: 1958, p. 79.

36. White, *op. cit.*, pp. 279-88.

37. *Ibid.*, p. 288.

38. *Ibid.*, p. 299.

39. Brandt, "The Qualified Attitude Method" in *Ethical Theory*, Prentice-Hall: Englewood Cliffs, N.J., 1959, pp. 241-69.

THREE: DECIDING WHO I AM

1. In trying to express their enthusiasm for Greek philosophy, Clement of Alexandria, Origen, and Gregory Thaumaturgus frequently expounded on this theme. See, for example, the latter's funeral oration for Origen in Anne Fremantle, *The Treasury of Early Christianity*, The Viking Press: New York, 1953, pp. 70-78. See also *The Ante-Nicene Fathers*, vol. II, Roberts, Donaldson, Coxe (eds.), Charles Scribner's Sons: New York, 1904, Introduction, and *ibid.*, vol. VI, pp. 21-39.

2. For the difference between knowledge of things considered in themselves and knowledge that relates things to observers, see Lonergan, *Insight*, pp. 291-96, 538-47, etc. For knowledge of oneself as subject, see his *De Constitutione Christi Ontologica et Psychologica*, Gregorian University Press: Rome, 1957, and his "Christ as Subject: A Reply," *Gregorianum*, 40 (1959), pp. 242-70.

3. Aristotle's reflections on understanding include these points (emphasis added): "Since everything is a possible object of understanding, mind in order . . . to know must be free of all admixture" (*On the Soul*, 429a, 19-20). "Mind is mind because it can *become* all things" (430a, 14-15). "Knowing in act *is identical with* its object" (430a, 20). "In every case the mind which is actively understanding *is* the object which it understands" (431b, 17-18).

4. See Sidney Hook's arguments in "The New Failure of Nerve," *The Quest for Being*, pp. 73-94, and *The Paradoxes of Freedom*, University of California Press: Berkeley, Calif., 1962, esp. pp. 1-22.

See also Stephen Toulmin, *Reason in Ethics*, Cambridge University Press: Cambridge, England, 1960, esp. pp. 202-21.

5. Barnes & Noble: New York, 1960, esp. pp. 42-61, 135-53 (on mental occurrences), pp. 154-98 (on self-knowledge), pp. 280-319 (on intellect).

6. Edited by Basil Mitchell, Beacon Press: Boston, Mass., 1957, "The Soul," pp. 132-48.

7. See Lonergan, "Christ as Subject," *op. cit.*

8. See my "An Empirically Controlled Metaphysics," *International Philosophical Quarterly*, 4 (1964), pp. 267-82.

9. *The Myth of Sisyphus*, Random House (Vintage Book): New York, 1960, pp. 38-39.

10. Alfred A. Knopf: New York, 1962, pp. 277-78.

11. See Lucas, in *Faith and Logic*, esp. pp. 140-48.

12. On the importance of "recollection," see Gabriel Marcel, "On the Ontological Mystery," *The Philosophy of Existentialism*, Citadel Press: New York, 1961.

13. For the concept of "inverse insight," see Lonergan, *Insight*, pp. 19-25, and for its applicability to statistical methods, *ibid.*, pp. 54-58, etc.

14. *Ibid.*, pp. 20-21, 229-32, 628-29, 666-67, 689-90.

15. The fundamental response of Aquinas to the platonic Averroës was the observation: "A man sometimes understands." See Lonergan, *Verbum* articles, *Theological Studies*, 10 (1949), p. 391. For the basic difference between a theory of knowing that understands intelligence in terms of *a subject confronting an object* (and that accordingly poses the epistemological problem as the problem of getting *from* the subject *to* the object), and of one that understands intelligence as *a subject in fact one with objects* (and that accordingly poses the epistemological problem as a matter of lived fact), see *ibid.*, pp. 359-66 and 388-93.

16. See Lucas, *op. cit.*, pp. 142-43.

17. For the concept of the "virtually unconditioned," see Lonergan, *Insight*, pp. 280-81, 340-45, 707-13, etc. For a comparison with Kant's "unconditioned," see *ibid.*, pp. 340-41, 641. (Note the changes in the treatment of Kant in the second edition.)

18. See J. L. Austin, "Other Minds," *Logic and Language*, 2nd series, *op. cit.*, esp. pp. 135-58, on the problems of certainty and error.

19. See my "The Philosophical Roots of Religious Ecumenism," to appear in the *Journal of Ecumenical Studies*.

20. See Lonergan, *Insight*, *op. cit.*, pp. 249-54, 291-96, 319, etc.

21. "Without [the pure, unrestricted drive to understand] there would be no real meaning for such phrases as scientific disinterestedness, scientific detachment, scientific impartiality. Inasmuch as this intellectual drive is dominant . . . in that measure the scientific observer becomes an incarnation of inquiring intelligence . . . ." *Ibid.*, p. 74.

22. Frederick E. Crowe, S.J., "Complacency and Concern," *Theological Studies, op. cit.*

23. The Viking Press: New York, 1960, pp. 90-91.

24. See note 19, *supra.*

25. Blackwell: Oxford, 1958.

26. *Insight, op. cit.*, pp. 4, 9, *passim.*

FOUR: WHAT DO I MEAN BY "GOD"?

1. See Kai Nielsen, "The Myth of Natural Law," *Law and Philosophy*, Sidney Hook, ed., New York University Press: New York, 1964, p. 139.

2. *The Basis of Belief*, Prentice-Hall (Hawthorn Book): Englewood Cliffs, N.J., 1961, pp. 53-66, esp. pp. 60-61. Dom Illtyd's survey of a usually overlooked tradition is a fruitful introduction to the problem.

3. See *Spirit as Inquiry*, "Studies in Honor of Bernard Lonergan," *Continuum*, 2 (1964), pp. 308-552.

4. See Chapter Two, *supra*, pp. 69-74.

5. See Chapter One, *supra*, pp. 39-44.

6. Kegley and Bretall, eds., *op. cit.*, p. 36.

7. *Ibid.*, pp. 36-37.

8. *Ibid.*, p. 37.

9. *Ibid.*

10. *Ibid.*, p. 40.

11. *Ibid.*

12. *Ibid.*, p. 41.

13. *Ibid.*, p. 432.

14. *Ibid.*

15. *Ibid.*

16. *Ibid.*, p. 433.

17. *Ibid.*

18. *Ibid.*, p. 36.

19. *Ibid.*

20. See P. Hoenen, *op. cit.*, and Joseph Maréchal, *Le Point de départ de la Metaphysique*, Desclée de Brouwer: Paris, 1949; B. Lonergan, *Verbum* articles, *op. cit.*

21. See G. E. M. Anscombe, "Aristotle and the Sea Battle," *Mind,* 65 (1956), esp. pp. 13-15, and David Burrell, "Aristotle and 'Future Contingencies,'" *Philosophical Studies* (Maynooth), 13 (1964), pp. 37-52. See also J. J. C. Smart, "The Existence of God," *New Essays in Philosophical Theology, op. cit.,* esp. pp. 44-46.

22. A translation of Tillich's ontological terms into cognitional terms seems to be possible. After such translation, ontological statements can be subjected to empirical scrutiny. ("Empirical" is here understood as referring primarily to cognitional, secondarily to sensory, experience.)

23. See B. Lonergan, "Metaphysics as Horizon," *Gregorianum,* 44 (1963), pp. 307-18; reprinted in *The Current* (Harvard-Radcliffe Club), 5 (1964), pp. 6-23.

24. See St. John of the Cross, *The Ascent of Mt. Carmel, The Dark Night of the Soul*; see also Maritain's excursus on St. John of the Cross in *The Degrees of Knowledge,* Geoffrey Bles: London, 1959, pp. 310-83.

25. Some readers will object to such a nonhistorical approach. God became man in Jesus Christ, they will insist, precisely to allow our imaginations, our sensibilities, and our craving for the factual to take a firm historical grip upon a concrete personality and upon actual events. Moreover, they will insist, the religious person correctly derives imaginative guidance from the language, symbols, rituals, and traditions of his historic community. Thus one ought not to "demythologize" oneself out of one's historical skin; it is good to be an incarnate man rather than a platonic spirit. Nevertheless, these same readers will be quick to admit that, in the end, the God who reveals himself *through* history, sense knowledge, and imagination, transcends these instruments of his revelation.

Since our present inquiry, however, abstracts from commitment to any one historical tradition in order to concentrate upon human intentionality, which is analytically prior to historical facts, conceptions, or traditions, it seems proper to emphasize the transcendence and hiddenness of God, on the one hand, and the unspecified hunger of man's intelligence, on the other. No Christian or Jew will be satisfied that our present inquiry adequately and fully expresses his *faith.* But we have clung steadfastly to our resolve to sort out, first, the problems of *belief,* which are philosophical and, in one sense at least, prior to problems of concrete, historical faith. Christian and Jewish faith have much more to propose in interpreting human life than our inquiry considers. But we are asking about the root, or the seedbed, of these religious proposals—about their foundation in men's normal, natural, and statistically frequent hunger for God—rather than about their further articulation under the grace and inspiration of God working in history.

26. Blackwell: Oxford, 1961, pp. 117-18.

27. *Ibid.*, pp. 109-10.

28. *Ibid.*, p. 117.

29. *Religious Experience and Truth*, New York University Press: New York, 1961, p. 64.

30. *Ibid.*, p. 63.

31. In "The New Failure of Nerve," *The Quest for Being*, St. Martin's Press: New York, 1961, p. 93.

32. In "Modern Knowledge and the Concept of God," *ibid.*, p. 120.

33. Thomas Aquinas, *In 1 Div. Nom.* 1, 27, and 29; *In Lib. de Causis* 6; *In 4 Metaph.* 12, 680. See also David Burrell, "Aquinas on Naming God," *Theological Studies*, 24 (1963), pp. 183-212.

34. See Part VI, "Theology and Falsification," *New Essays in Philosophical Theology, op. cit.*, pp. 96-130. See also Frederick Ferré, *Language, Logic, and God*, Harper & Row: New York, 1961, esp. pp. 146-66.

35. See David Burrell, *op. cit.* (n. 33, *supra*), and "Analogy and Judgment," *Spirit as Inquiry, op. cit.*, pp. 434-46.

36. See Lonergan, *Insight, op. cit.*, pp. 53-68, 97-100, etc.

37. *Ibid.*, pp. 123-34, 171-72, 210-11 ff.

38. *Ibid.*, pp. 19-25.

39. See J. Maritain, "The Meaning of Contemporary Atheism," *The Range of Reason*, Charles Scribner's Sons: New York, 1952, pp. 103-17, esp. pp. 103-5.

40. See Malcolm Lowrie, *Kierkegaard*, 2 vols., Harper & Row (Torchbook): New York, 1962, on Kierkegaard's notions, and personal growth through, the ethical, the aesthetical, and the religious spheres: esp. pp. 150-67, 232-90, 391-449.

FIVE: DECIDING WHETHER TO BELIEVE

1. See, e.g., R. M. Chisholm, *Perceiving*, Cornell University Press: Ithaca, N.Y., 1957; Roderick Firth, "Phenomenalism," American Philosophical Association Suppl. Vol., 1952, *Science, Language and Human Rights*, pp. 1-20; and W. V. Quine, *Word and Object*, The M.I.T. Press: Cambridge, Mass., 1960, pp. 234-39, etc.

2. See Bernard Lonergan, *Insight, op. cit.*, chap. 8, pp. 245-70.

3. See Sidney Hook, *The Quest for Being, op. cit.,* pp. 227-28, for praise of a philosophy "wider and more precious than science." In this connection, see Henry David Aiken, "Sidney Hook as Philosopher," *Commentary,* 33 (1962), pp. 143-51; also, Morton V. White, "Beyond Positivism and Pragmatism," *Toward Reunion in Philosophy, op. cit.,* pp. 279-88.

4. See Lonergan, note 2, *supra.*

5. Lonergan, *Insight, op. cit.,* on "the scotosis of the dramatic subject," pp. 191-203.

6. Sidney Hook, for example, calls himself a "skeptical God-seeker." *The Quest for Being, op. cit.,* p. 115. In similar fashion, Wallace I. Matson has thought it worth expending the energy required to write his *The Existence of God,* though he does not understand why to some persons God matters more than anything else, and though he writes about the issue as would a visitor to a strange land, *op. cit.,* p. 245.

7. In *New Essays in Philosophical Theology, op. cit.,* pp. 74-75.

8. See W. V. Quine, *From a Logical Point of View, op. cit.,* p. 44.

9. See Chapter Seven, n. 11.

10. See Martin D'Arcy, "The Search for the Self" in *No Absent God,* Harper & Row: New York, 1962, pp. 72-84, esp. his reminder that God, according to St. John, knows each man by name (p. 75). See also D'Arcy's discussion of Ryle on the self, pp. 100-15.

11. In *New Essays in Philosophical Theology, op. cit.,* pp. 28-46.

12. *Ibid.,* p. 46.

13. *Ibid.* Smart, like Matson (*op. cit.*), seems to commit an historical error in assimilating the "five ways" of Aquinas to the "three traditional arguments" of later rationalistic thought. Nearly every key word in the discussion—"necessary," for example—has changed its meaning in the centuries intervening between Aquinas and Wolfe. For a start toward a more accurate historical view of Aquinas, see Edward Sillem, *Ways of Thinking About God,* Sheed & Ward: New York, 1961, and Thomas Gornall, S.J., *A Philosophy of God,* Sheed & Ward: New York, 1962. For an analysis of basic differences between Aquinas and Kant, see Joseph Maréchal, *Le point de depart de la metaphysique,* Vol. V, *Le Thomisme devant la philosophie critique, op. cit.,* esp. pp. 564-97, and David Burrell, "Kant and Philosophical Knowledge," *The New Scholasticism,* 38 (1964), pp. 189-213, esp. pp. 206-13.

14. See Jean Daniélou, *The Scandal of Truth,* Helicon Press: Baltimore, Md., 1962, pp. 1-7 and *passim.*

15. See my "A Key to Aristotle's 'Substance,'" *Philosophy and Phenomenological Research*, 24 (1963), pp. 1-19.

16. See the review by W. V. Quine of J. J. C. Smart's *Philosophy and Scientific Realism* in *New York Review of Books*, July 9, 1964. Quine writes (p. 3): "Physics investigates the essential nature of the world, and biology describes a local bump. Psychology, human psychology, describes a bump on a bump." Yet human psychology is the source of science, philosophy, and "scientific realism." It may also be the key to all else. At issue here is whether one takes physics or psychology to be the radical factor in one's own acts of understanding. At issue is one's interpretation of one's own identity.

SIX: GOD OR EVIL

1. In *Reason and Conduct*, Alfred A. Knopf: New York, 1962, p. 175.

2. *Ibid.*, p. 176.

3. *Ibid.*, p. 179.

4. *Ibid.*

5. *Ibid.*, p. 178.

6. *Ibid.*, p. 177.

7. *Ibid.*, p. 183.

8. *Ibid.*, pp. 181-86. I think Mr. Aiken is mistaken, however, in basing the notion of "person" upon external moral relationships, thus defining personality functionally. Such a legal, juridical manner of proceeding leads to formalism, as chastened Catholics are well aware. The notion of personality is better defined, it appears, through the experiences of self-awareness, the drive to understand, reflection, and decision. God may be conceived as somehow capable of these experiences.

9. *Ibid.*, p. 190.

10. *Ibid.*, pp. 175 ff.

11. J. O. Urmson, "On Grading," in Flew, *Logic and Language*, Second Series, *op. cit.*, pp. 159-86.

12. See Mary Warnock, *Ethics Since 1900*, Oxford University Press: London, 1960.

13. *Op. cit.*, p. 82.

14. *Ibid.*

15. See B. Lonergan in *Spirit As Inquiry, op. cit.*, p. 542.

16. Thus Aristotle reverses the Socratic criterion for the good man. It is not correct knowing which is primary, but correct willing; i.e., a will whose intention is to do as understanding directs. It is the man

of practical wisdom, not the isolated intelligence, that is the criterion of moral action. Concrete experience is more subtle than intelligence can articulate, and a moral "sense," a good "instinct," "good will," affords an accuracy, speed, and flexibility in concrete, contingent action which intelligence can later scrutinize and evaluate, but cannot ordinarily precede. See *Nichomachean Ethics*: "The truth in practical matters is discerned from the facts of life; for these are the decisive factor" (1179*a*, 17-20). "With regard to virtue, then, it is not enough to know . . ." (1179*b*, 1-2). See also Bk. 6, chs. 5-13, and especially 1142*a*, 13-30; 1143*b*, 11-14; and, on the error of Socrates, 1144*b*, 19-30.

17. Jacques Maritain has long emphasized the importance of the first moral choice of the good. See his *Approaches to God*, Harper & Row: New York, 1954, pp. 92-104; *The Range of Reason, op. cit.*, chap. 6.

18. See Teilhard de Chardin, *The Phenomenon of Man*, Harper & Row: New York, 1959.

19. In *Three Essays on Religion*, Longman's, Green & Co.: London, 1874, I, III (pp. 37-38; 176-77). I was led to these passages by James Collins, *God in Modern Philosophy*, Bruce Publishing Co.: Milwaukee, Wisc., 1959, p. 293. Parenthetically, let me add that I am much indebted to the erudition and acumen of Professor Collins. Still, I find the judgment of perception which to him seems basic in the question of discovering God less telling than an analysis of first awareness, second awareness, the drive to understand, and critical reflection. For these are basic in the judgment of perception, and in every other human judgment.

20. *Op. cit.*, p. 194.

21. For the general theorem of God's operation and man's cooperation in good, and man's sole claim to his own sins, see the historical study by Bernard Lonergan, "The Thought of St. Thomas Aquinas on *Gratia Operans*," *Theological Studies*, 2 (1941), pp. 290-325; 3 (1942), pp. 69-86, 375-406, 533-75.

SEVEN: AN EFFECTIVE HUMANISM

1. Ignace Lepp, "The Church and Atheists," *The Commonweal*, 81 (October 16, 1964), pp. 88-90.

2. *The Essence of Christianity*, Harper & Row (Torchbook): New York, 1957. Quoted by Karl Barth in his introduction, p. xi.

3. *Ibid.*

4. *Religious Experience and Truth, op. cit.*, p. 63.

5. See *supra*, pp. 69-74.

6. In his reply to his critics in volume II, *Library of Living Theology*, Kegley and Bretall (eds.), *op. cit.*, p. 434.

7. *Ibid.*

8. The concrete political vision of Jacques Maritain in *True Humanism*, Geoffrey Bles: London, 1954, is a sample of what can be done; the work of Reinhold Niebuhr is less visionary, but more detailed.

9. Generically, there are three approaches to religion: through reason, through decision (will), through feeling. Triads of names—like Leibniz, Kierkegaard, Schleiermacher; or Tillich, Barth, Scheler—exemplify these tendencies. Our effort throughout this inquiry has been "to put Humpty-Dumpty together again," by employing an interpretation of reason which is not the "mere reason" of post-Cartesian philosophy but a dynamic and complex drive. This drive begins to operate by (at least an implicit) decision concerning its own canons of operation, and these canons are arrived at and modified by the interaction of inquiry and experience. Intelligence begins in a decision, decision is suffused with intelligence, and intelligence and decision are called for and challenged by experience. Not "mere mind" but the entire person understands and knows; decision is not a blind leap; and experience shapes and is shaped by the attention, goals, and inquiries of the person. The stress of this inquiry upon intelligence should not, then, be misconstrued as rationalistic. For we have been dealing with intelligence as "drive" and "light," not intelligence as generator of concepts and logical connections. This dynamic life of intelligence seems to be the root of religion, the foundation of ecumenism, the characterizing note of the human spirit, man's defense against obscurantism and fanaticism, and the empirical base by which men intend to name the hidden and (strictly) inconceivable God.

10. *Religious Experience and Truth, op. cit.*, 62.

11. For a beginning in the study of the psychology of unbelief, see Ignace Lepp, *Atheism in Our Time*, The Macmillan Company (paperback): New York, 1964, and H. C. Rümke, *The Psychology of Unbelief*, Sheed & Ward: New York, 1963; Rockliff: London, 1952.

12. See William Lynch, S.J., *The Image Industries*, Sheed & Ward: New York, 1959; *The Integrating Mind*, Sheed & Ward: New York, 1962.

13. See my "The Gap Between Intellectuals and People," *A New Generation*, Herder & Herder: New York, 1964, pp. 107-20.

A SELECTED
BIBLIOGRAPHY

(Not all books and articles cited in the text are included; and a few included here have not been directly cited in the text.)

Aiken, Henry David, *Reason and Conduct*, Alfred A. Knopf: New York, 1962.

Anscombe, G. E. M., *Intention*, Basil Blackwell: Oxford, 1958.

——, and P. T. Geach, *Three Philosophers*, Basil Blackwell: Oxford, 1961.

Aquinas, Thomas, *Summa Theologica*, Marietti (ed.): Turin, 1950.

Aristotle, the *Nichomachean Ethics*, in *The Basic Works of Aristotle*, Richard McKeon (ed.); also trans. by J. A. K. Thompson, Penguin Paperbacks: London, 1963.

Ayer, Alfred Jules, *Language, Truth, and Logic*, Dover Publications: New York (n. d. listed).

——, *The Problem of Knowledge*, Penguin Books: Harmondsworth, Middlesex, 1957.

Baillie, John, *Our Knowledge of God*, Charles Scribner's Sons: New York, 1959.

Balthasar, Hans Urs von, *Science, Religion and Christianity*, Burns, Oates and Washbourne: London, 1958.

Bartley, William Warren III, *The Retreat to Commitment*, Alfred A. Knopf: New York, 1962.

Blackstone, William T., *The Problem of Religious Knowledge*, Prentice-Hall, Inc. (paperback): Englewood Cliffs, N.J., 1963.

Brandt, Richard B., *Ethical Theory*, Prentice-Hall: Englewood Cliffs, N.J., 1959.

Buber, Martin, *I and Thou*, Charles Scribner's Sons: New York, 1958.

Burrell, David, "Aquinas on Naming God," *Theological Studies* (24) 1963, pp. 183-212.

——, "Kant and Philosophical Knowledge," *The New Scholasticism* (38) 1964, pp. 189-213.

Callahan, Daniel, *Honesty in the Church*, Charles Scribner's Sons: New York, 1965.

Camus, Albert, *The Myth of Sisyphus*, Random House (Vintage Book): New York, 1960.

——, *The Fall*, Alfred A. Knopf: New York, 1961.

Chenu, Rev. M. D., O.P., *Toward Understanding St. Thomas*, Henry Regnery: Chicago, 1964.

Chisholm, Roderick M., *Perceiving: A Philosophical Study*, Cornell University Press: Ithaca, N.Y., 1957.

Collins, James, *God in Modern Philosophy*, Henry Regnery: Chicago, 1959.

——, *Three Paths in Philosophy*, Henry Regnery: Chicago, 1962.

Crowe, Frederick E., "Complacency and Concern in the Thought of St. Thomas," *Theological Studies*, 20 (1959).

—— (ed.), *Spirit as Inquiry—Studies in Honor of Bernard Lonergan, S.J., Continuum*, vol. II, no. 3 (Autumn, 1964).

Daniélou, Jean, *God and the Ways of Knowing*, Harcourt, Brace & World (Meridian Book): New York, 1957.

——, *The Scandal of Truth*, Helicon Press: Baltimore, Md., 1962.

D'Arcy, Martin C., S.J., *The Nature of Belief*, Clonmore and Reynolds: Dublin, 1958.

——, *No Absent God*, Harper & Row: New York, 1962.

Deane, S. W., *Saint Anselm—Basic Writings*, Open Court Publishing Co.: La Salle, Ill., 1962.

Donceel, J. F., S.J., *Natural Theology*, Sheed & Ward: New York, 1962.

Eliot, T. S., *Selected Essays*, Harcourt, Brace & World: New York, 1950.

Ferré, Frederick, *Language, Logic, and God*, Harper & Row: New York, 1961.

Feuerbach, Ludwig, *The Essence of Christianity*, Harper & Row: New York, 1957.

Flew, A. G. N., *Logic and Language*, 2nd Series, Basil Blackwell: Oxford, 1959.

—— (ed.), *Logic and Language*, 1st Series, Basil Blackwell: Oxford, 1960.

——, and Alasdair MacIntyre (eds.), *New Essays in Philosophical Theology*, SCM Press: London, 1958.

Fromm, Erich, *The Art of Loving*, Harper & Row: New York, 1956.

Gallagher, Kenneth T., *The Philosophy of Gabriel Marcel*, Fordham University Press: New York, 1962.

Gilson, Etienne, *Elements of Christian Philosophy*, Doubleday & Co.: New York, 1960.

Gleason, Robert W., S.J., *The Search for God*, Sheed & Ward: New York, 1964.

Gornall, Thomas, S.J., *A Philosophy of God*, Sheed & Ward: New York, 1962.

Graham, Dom Aelred, *Zen Catholicism*, Harcourt, Brace & World: New York, 1963.

Hampshire, Stuart, *Thought and Action*, The Viking Press: New York, 1960.

Hare, R. M., *The Language of Morals*, Oxford University Press: London, 1952.

Heer, Friedrich and Szczesny, Gerhard, *Glaube und Unglaube*, Paul List Verlag (paperback): München, 1962.

Heschel, Abraham Joshua, *God in Search of Man*, Harcourt, Brace & World (Meridian Book) and The Jewish Publication Society of America: New York, 1961.

Hick, John (ed.), *The Existence of God*, The Macmillan Company: New York, 1964.

Hoenen, Peter, S.J., *Reality and Judgment According to St. Thomas*, Henry Regnery: Chicago, 1952.

Hook, Sidney, *The Quest for Being*, St. Martin's Press: New York, 1961.

—— (ed.), *Law and Philosophy*, New York University Press: New York, 1964.

—— (ed.), *Religious Experience and Truth*, New York University Press: New York, 1961.

Horney, Karen, *Self-Analysis*, W. W. Norton: New York, 1942.

Hume, David, *Dialogues Concerning Natural Religion*, Hafner Publishing Co.: New York, 1961.

St. John of the Cross, *The Complete Works*, E. Allison Peers (ed.), 3 vols., Newman Press: Westminster, Maryland, 1946.

Jolivet, Régis, *The God of Reason*, Prentice-Hall (Hawthorne Book): Englewood Cliffs, N.J., 1960.

Kant, Immanuel, *Critique of Pure Reason*, The Macmillan Company: New York, 1958.

——, *Religion Within the Limits of Reason Alone*, Harper & Row: New York, 1960.

Kaufmann, Walter, *Critique of Religion and Philosophy*, Doubleday & Company (Anchor Book): New York, 1961.

——, *The Faith of a Heretic*, Doubleday & Company: New York, 1961.

Kegley, Charles W., and Robert W. Bretall (eds.), *Reinhold Niebuhr, His Religious, Social, and Political Thought*, Library of Living Theology, vol. 2, The Macmillan Company: New York, 1956.

Kohler, Dr. Wolfgang, *Gestalt Psychology*, Liverwright Publishing Corporation (Mentor Book): New York, 1947.

Lacroix, Jean, *Le Sens de l'Athéisme Moderne*, Casterman: Tournai, Paris, 1958.

Lamont, Corliss, *The Illusion of Immortality*, Philosophical Library: New York, 1959.

Lepp, Ignace, *Atheism in Our Time*, The Macmillan Company: New York, 1964.

——, *The Christian Failure*, The Newman Press: Westminster, Md., 1962.

Le Roy, Édouard, *Le Probleme de Dieu*, Choureau: Paris, 1929.

Lewis, C. S., *The Abolition of Man*, The Crowell-Collier Publishing Company (Collier Book): New York, 1962.

Lonergan, Bernard J. F., *Insight: A Study of Human Understanding*, Longman's, Green & Co.: London, 1958 (2nd ed.).

Lovejoy, Arthur O., *The Great Chain of Being*, Harper & Row, (Torchbook): New York, 1936.

Lowrie, Walter, D.D., *Kierkegaard*, 2 vols., Harper & Row, (Torchbook): New York, 1962.

Lubac, Henri de, S.J., *The Drama of Atheistic Humanism*, Harcourt, Brace & World (Meridian Book): New York, 1963.

Luijpen, William A., O.S.A., *Existential Phenomenology*, Duquesne Studies Philosophical Series, vol. 12, Duquesne University Press: Pittsburgh, Pa., 1960.

MacGregor, Geddes, *Introduction to Religious Philosophy*, Houghton Mifflin Company: Boston, 1959.

MacIntyre, Alasdair C., *Difficulties in Christian Belief*, SCM Press: London, 1961.

Malcolm, Norman, *Ludwig Wittgenstein, A Memoir*, Oxford University Press: London, 1959.

Marcel, Gabriel, *Creative Fidelity*, Farrar, Straus & Company: New York, 1964.

——, *The Mystery of Being*, 2 vols., Henry Regnery: Chicago, 1960.

——, *The Philosophy of Existentialism*, Citadel Press: New York, 1961.

Maréchal, Joseph, S.J., *Le Point de Départ de la Métaphysique*, Cahier V "Le Thomisme devant la Philosophie Critique," l'edition Universelle: Bruxelles, Desclée de Brouwer: Paris, 1949.

Maritain, Jacques, *Approaches to God*, Harper & Row: New York, 1954.

——, *Existence and the Existent*, Doubleday & Company, (Image Book): New York, 1957.

——, *The Range of Reason*, Charles Scribner's Sons: New York, 1952.

——, *True Humanism*, Geoffrey Bles: London, 1954.

Marty, Martin E., *Varieties of Unbelief*, Holt, Rinehart and Winston: New York, 1964.

Mascall, E. L., *Existence and Analogy*, Longman's, Green and Co.: London, 1949.

Mitchell, Basil (ed.), *Faith and Logic*, Beacon Press: Boston, 1957.

Murray, John Courtney, S.J., *The Problem of God*, Yale University Press: New Haven, Conn., 1964.

Newman, John Henry Cardinal, *The Grammar of Assent*, Doubleday and Company (Image Book): New York, 1958.

Niebuhr, Reinhold, *Faith and History*, Charles Scribner's Sons: New York, 1949.

——, *The Nature and Destiny of Man*, 2 vols., Charles Scribner's Sons: New York, 1964.

——, *The Self and the Dramas of History*, Charles Scribner's Sons: New York, 1955.

Niebuhr, Richard R., *Schleiermacher on Christ and Religion*, Charles Scribner's Sons: New York, 1964.

Ong, Walter J., S.J., *The Barbarian Within*, The Macmillan Company: New York, 1962.

Ortega y Gasset, *What is Philosophy?* W. W. Norton: New York, 1960.

Otto, Rudolf, *The Idea of the Holy*, Oxford University Press (Galaxy Book): New York, 1958.

Pascal, Blaise, *Pensées*, E. P. Dutton & Co.: New York, 1958.

Passmore, John, *A Hundred Years of Philosophy*, Duckworth: London, 1962.

Pears, D. F. (ed.), *The Nature of Metaphysics*, Macmillan & Co.: London, 1962.

Pepper, Stephen C., *World Hypotheses*, University of California Press, Berkeley and Los Angeles, 1961.

Pieper, Josef, *Belief and Faith*, Random House (Pantheon Book): New York, 1963.

——, *Guide to Thomas Aquinas*, Random House (Pantheon Book): New York, 1962.

Polanyi, Michael, *Personal Knowledge—Towards a Post-Critical Philosophy*, University of Chicago Press: Chicago, 1960.

Price, H. H., *Perception*, Methuen & Co.: London, 1961.

Quine, Willard Van Orman, *From a Logical Point of View*, Harvard University Press: Cambridge, Mass., 1953.

——, *Methods of Logic*, Holt, Rinehart & Winston: New York, 1959.

——, *Word and Object*, The Technology Press of M.I.T. and John Wiley & Sons: New York, 1960.

Ramsey, Ian T., *Religious Language*, The Macmillan Company: New York, 1963.

Robinson, John A. T., *Honest to God*, The Westminster Press: Philadelphia, Pa., 1963.

Rümke, H. C., *The Psychology of Unbelief*, Rockliff Publishing Corp.: London, 1952; Sheed & Ward: New York, 1963.

Ryle, Gilbert, *The Concept of Mind*, Barnes & Noble: New York, 1960.

Sartre, Jean-Paul, *The Words*, George Braziller: New York, 1964.

Scharlemann, Robert P., *Thomas Aquinas and John Gerhard*, Yale University Press: New Haven, Conn., 1964.

Scheler, Max, *On the Eternal in Man*, Harper & Row: New York, 1960.

Schleiermacher, Friedrich, *On Religion*, Harper & Row (Torchbook): New York, 1958.

Sillem, Edward, *Ways of Thinking About God*, Sheed & Ward: New York, 1961.

Skinner, B. F., *Science and Human Behavior*, The Macmillan Company: New York, 1953.

Smart, Ninian, *Reasons and Faith*, Routledge and Kegan Paul: London, 1958.

Strawson, P. F., *Individuals*, Methuen: London, 1961.

Suhard, Emmanuel Cardinal, *The Church Today: Growth or Decline?*, Fides Press: Notre Dame, Ind., 1948.

Teilhard de Chardin, Pierre, *The Divine Milieu*, Harper & Row: New York, 1960.

——, *The Phenomenon of Man*, Harper & Row: New York, 1959.

Thielicke, Helmut, *Nihilism*, Harper & Row: New York, 1961.

Tillich, Paul, *The Courage to Be*, Yale University Press: New Haven, Conn., 1963.

——, *Systematic Theology*, vol. I, University of Chicago Press: Chicago, 1963.

Toulmin, Stephen, *The Place of Reason in Ethics*, Cambridge University Press: London, 1960.

——, Ronald W. Hepburn, and Alasdair MacIntyre, *Metaphysical Beliefs*, SCM Press: London, 1957.

Tresmontant, Claude, *Toward the Knowledge of God*, Helicon Press: Baltimore, 1961.

Trethowan, Illtyd, O.S.B., *The Basis of Belief*, Prentice-Hall (Hawthorne Book). Englewood Cliffs, N.J., 1961.

Warnock, Mary, *Ethics Since 1900*, Oxford University Press: London, 1960.

Weigel, Gustave, S.J., *The Modern God*, The Macmillan Company: New York, 1963.

White, Morton, *Toward Reunion in Philosophy*, Harvard University Press: Cambridge, Mass., 1956.

White, Victor, O.P., *God the Unknown*, The Harvill Press: London, 1956.

Wittgenstein, Ludwig, *Philosophical Investigations*, Blackwell: Oxford, 1958.

——, *Tractatus Logico-Philosophicus*, Routledge and Kegan Paul: London, 1960.

Woozley, A. D., *Theory of Knowledge*, Hutchinson University Library: London, 1962.

Zaehner, R. C., *Matter and Spirit*, Harper & Row: New York, 1963.

INDEX